Film as Cultural Artifact

D1282241

Film as Cultural Artifact

Mathew P. John

Fortress Press
Minneapolis

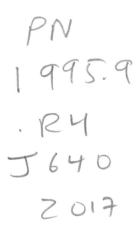

FILM AS CULTURAL ARTIFACT
Religious Criticism of World Cinema

Cover image: Photographer: Maysam Makhmalbaf/Stray Dogs/Marziyeh
Meshkiny/ Makhmalbaf Film House/ www.makhmalbaf.com.

Cover design: Laurie Ingram

Print ISBN: 978-1-5064-2169-8
eBook ISBN: 978-1-5064-2170-4

The paper used in this publication meets the minimum requirements of American
National Standard for Information Sciences — Permanence of Paper for Printed
Library Materials, ANSI Z329.48-1984.

Manufactured in the U.S.A.

This book was produced using Pressbooks.com, and PDF rendering was done by
PrinceXML.

To

Hannah and Emma

You are the stars

that add music, dance, and color

to the wonderful Bollywood movie

our life has become.

Contents

Foreword

Robert K. Johnston

Ten years ago, a dozen senior scholars of "theology and film," together with several leading filmmakers, came together to discuss what should be the emerging foci in theology and film studies over the next decade. The consultation was hosted by the Reel Spirituality Institute at Fuller Theological Seminary in Pasadena, California, and was generously funded by the Henry Luce Foundation, Michael Gilligan, president. Out of this three-year process came six recommendations, which were published as *Reframing Theology and Film: New Focus for an Emerging Discipline* (Baker, 2007):

1. The need methodologically to move beyond a largely "literary" paradigm, recognizing the importance of image and sound when uncovering the power and meaning of a film story.
2. The need for studies in theology and film to broaden their film selection beyond Hollywood, embracing world cinema as equal and necessary artistic texts.
3. The need to extend the number of conversation partners beyond simply those in film studies and those in theology, reaching out in particular to the arts and social sciences.
4. The need to engage not only a film's creators (auteur criticism), but also the film's viewers (reception criticism) in order to have a fuller understanding of a film's religious meaning and significance.

5. The need to not shy away from normative criticism. Or to put it in the positive, the need to bring theology into the dialogue with film as a full partner.
6. The need to make better use of a wide variety of theological traditions.

What is remarkable about this book, *Film as Cultural Artifact*, is how creatively it engages most of these needed, new directions in theology and film research. Not only has Mathew John given us a model for engaging with world cinema, he has done so by interlacing insight from visual anthropology. (He is both an ethnographer and a student of film—an anthropologist and a filmmaker.) He not only has provided a model for what auteur criticism can contribute to the critical discussion of theology and film, he also has shown what a film's social reception can add to its theological meaning. (As Margaret Miles says, "Meaning is negotiated between the spectator and the film.") And John is conversant not only with the Christian tradition, but also with the multiple religious traditions that make up India's religious landscape.

John has provided a fascinating, thick description of the Elements Trilogy by Deepa Mehta that opens readers' eyes to both its cultural and theological depth. Although I have often taught the film *Water* in my classes, I learned much from his thoughtful dialogue with these films—much about these movies, but also much about cultural exegesis. John has seen the importance of film to investigations of religion, and of religion to critical discussion of film. Film depictions can help religionists better explore a theology's emotional range and depth, and an understanding of a cultural context's religious commitments and beliefs can aid in understanding a film's power and meaning. A striking feature of Indian cinema is this intermingling of the religious and the cultural. As we move ever more strongly into postmodernity with its awakened sense of culture's spiritual and religious groundedness, John's study will provide a valuable model for us all in the importance of interlacing the artistic, the cultural, and the religious.

In my two decades of teaching theology and film, one of the most significant changes I have observed has been the increasingly warm reception given by my students to cinema from outside Hollywood. As John argues effectively, world cinema reminds us that Hollywood is only one expression of a wider phenomenon, no longer the standard through which to judge all else. My current students, for example, find the Japanese gem *Departures* to be their favorite movie in the class.

Whether Kieslowski's *Dekalogue* or Mehta's *Water*, whether Tykwer's *Run Lola Run* or the dystopic Korean film *Snowpiercer*, world cinema both captures my students' attention and reveals a depth of spirit that at times invites the Spirit.

Like the movies being discussed, this book will both entertain and inform. If you haven't seen Deepa Mehta's trilogy, it will make you want to put these movies on your Netflix list. If you have, it will make you want to see them again, so you might notice all that you missed the first time. Put your feet up and enjoy the read.

Robert K. Johnston
Author of *Reel Spirituality*
Professor of Theology and Culture, Fuller Theological Seminary

Acknowledgments

An anthropologist, an ethnomusicologist, and a theologian walk into a movie theater. . . . Does that sound like the beginning of a joke? It actually is not. I am describing a dream team of scholars—Daniel Shaw, Roberta King, and Robert Johnston—coming together on a summer afternoon to assess my research proposal on "cultural exegesis of film" at Fuller Theological Seminary (FTS) in Los Angeles.

It was the genesis of a passionate project, which demanded the best available expertise in the otherwise disconnected fields of cultural anthropology, film criticism, and theology. I am immensely grateful, not only for the intellectual contribution of these brilliant scholars to this project, but also for their unwavering patience and indulgent kindness, much of which I feel like I have shamelessly exploited during the course of my research.

I had the fortuitous privilege to have my favorite author and his gracious wife, Philip and Janet Yancey, as mentors and patrons in this project (and beyond). Thank you so much for incessantly and lavishly dispensing the "amazing grace" that you write so eloquently about!

I remember with a deep sense of gratitude Jack Costello, SJ, Dennis Ngien, and Andrew Stirling, three eminent scholars and teachers from my hometown Toronto, and Carol Christopher and Drew Logan, my closest colleagues and confidants at FTS, as they caringly and constantly nudged me to be persistent in my academic pursuit.

Not many funding agencies were sympathetic to my project, primarily because of its hybrid nature, but Someone Care Foundation (USA) and the Priscilla and Stanford Reid Trust (Canada) took a chance and extended gratuitous financial support to my research. Thank you for investing in this project.

I would also like to thank my literary agent, Pieter Kwant, for investing his time in a novice writer like me, and Sol Pineda, and Michael Gibson for enriching this work with prompt and professional editorial assistance.

Although scholarly pursuit is meant to be an intensely personal journey, my wife Joanne left her family, friends, and a flourishing professional career to walk with me on this long and winding road. Our children, Hannah and Emma, followed suit with equal grace and fortitude. Thank you for tolerating my temperaments, lifting my spirits up with the tenacity of motivational speakers, and above all, teaching me how to become a better human being with each passing day.

Introduction

Film plays a pivotal role in facilitating intercultural dialogue in our global village. The cinema of the world helps us understand and appreciate each other's cultural identity and promote harmony across the different cultures in our society. Film introduces us to the life of "the other" in an entertaining yet engaging fashion, creating cultural bridges that foster a sense of unity among our diversity.

Film is popularly described as a mirror of culture. But what is culture anyway? It is one of the multifaceted descriptors scholars have coined to categorize a number of interrelated observable phenomena in a society. Whichever way we choose to define culture, one of its primary components is religion—a belief and worldview system, which manifests itself in variety of forms such as mythology, rituals, symbols, and so on.

According to traditional views of (Western) academia, religious beliefs in a society are shaped by its cultural presuppositions. But in most parts of the world, cultural phenomena are filtered through the spectacles of religion. To do authentic religious criticism of film, therefore, one must interlace the methodologies of theological criticism with critical methods borrowed from the field of culture studies.

In this book, I posit that cultural anthropology and theology offer two distinct yet intrinsically connected theoretical frameworks to formulate a more holistic reading of religion from world cinema. I will propose an integrated methodology for religious criticism of film in which we look at religion as a subsystem of culture and observe how religious experiences depicted on the screen are mediated through the personal bias of the auteur and the context in which the film is produced.

We will consider Bollywood, the largest film industry in the world, as a test case for the study of world cinema. To test the authenticity of the methodology, we will perform a case study on the Elements Trilogy—*Fire* (1996), *Earth* (1999), and *Water* (2005), an acclaimed film series from "diasporic" Bollywood. The study consists of field research conducted in India using multiple methods such as participant observation, focus groups, and ethnographic interviews with local experts, including the writer/director of the trilogy, Ms. Deepa Mehta. The case study illustrates the workings of the proposed method in critiquing a film from the perspective of religion.

In the first chapter, we will examine religions' resemblance to film, as a narrative of culture. We will observe how film contributes to the religious sensibilities of the postmodern mind and establish the need for a new methodology for religious criticism of film, combining both cultural (functional) and theological (substantive) aspects of religion.

In the second chapter, we will establish a framework for theological criticism of film based on the many existing methodologies in this field. We will see that even a film with no explicit religious content can provide religion-like experiences for its viewers and initiate meaningful conversation between film and theology.

In the third chapter, I will propose a methodology for cultural exegesis of film, which decodes ethnographic data from the diegetic world of a film. The methodology uses an interlacing of (a) virtual participant observation, which assumes viewers' virtual interaction with the filmic world; (b) auteur criticism, which explores the subjectivity and reflectivity of the filmmaker; and (c) context criticism, which examines various cultural concerns within the context in which the film is produced, distributed, and consumed.

In the fourth chapter, I will define world cinema as a global process and present Bollywood as a test case to examine the re-presentation of religion in world cinema. We will also take a brief look at critical methods applied specifically to Bollywood films and industry practices characteristic of Indian film industry.

In the fifth chapter, I will introduce the Elements Trilogy as a case study. In the words of Deepa Mehta, the auteur of the film series, "The trilogy is about politics. *Fire* is about the politics of sexuality, *Earth* is about the politics of nationalism, and *Water* is about the politics of religion." Based on auteur criticism of the trilogy and my personal interview with Mehta, we will make a case for "diasporic Bollywood," a cultural space from which we can observe both etic and emic perspectives on religion in Bollywood film.

In the sixth chapter, we will analyze field research conducted in India using multiple methods, such as participant observation, focus groups, and ethnographic interviews. Comparing the ethnographic data gathered from the diegetic world of the film against the data collected from the actual field, we will examine how the depiction of the "religious" in film is influenced by the reflexivity of the filmmaker and the driving concerns of the filmmaking context.

In the seventh chapter, we will conduct a religious reading of the Elements Trilogy, examining its portrayal of religion from both "functional" and "substantive" perspectives. We will observe how cultural and theological themes are emerging from the film, demonstrating the efficacy of the new methodology in doing religious criticism of film.

India is a complex country, which consists of diverse people groups with different aesthetic, linguistic, and cultural identities. It is divided geographically into different states, all of which claim their own distinctive cultural heritage in the areas of art, dance, theater, music, language, and social customs. As Roy and Jhala observe, "These traditions have local, regional, national and international orbits. They work sometimes in concert and at other times in opposition to each other. This then is the rich Indian heritage which awaits systematic and concerted address by [visual] anthropologists" (1992: 20). Needless to mention, a comprehensive study of culture is practically impossible on account of the sheer volume of customs, traditions and varied forms of their practice in a country like India. Therefore in my case study, I will only discuss the themes emerging from the trilogy, which are considered representative of the totality of the contemporary Indian culture.

Although India is considered a pluralistic country from a religious perspective, Hindus form the majority population, and Hinduism shapes the primary worldview of the society. Hinduism itself is a pluralistic conglomerate of eclectic customs, traditions, and belief systems practiced across the country. However, we can identify certain pervading belief systems that are common to all sects of Hinduism, such as the belief in a universal spirit, reincarnation, and karmic worldview. For the purpose of this book, I consider "Indian culture" as a derivative of "Hindu culture" and treat these terms somewhat as analogues. As Dwyer puts it, "Hinduism is the invisible norm, the standard default position" (2006: 136).

The terms *cinema, film, movie,* and *motion picture* have been used interchangeably throughout this book in order to represent a full-length narrative motion picture that enacts a story, produced for the purpose of entertainment and distributed for the viewing of general public.

Even though all three films of the Elements Trilogy are considered in the case study, the research is limited to *Water* in order to avoid the field data being too exhaustive and cumbersome. This selection was made based on the fact that *Water* (a) is the final film of the series; (b) took more years to research and produce; (c) won more critical acclaim, including an Academy Award nomination; and (d) in Mehta's own words, deals with the politics of religion, which happens to be the focus of the book.

Thanks to the emergence of online social networks and Internet-based distribution companies, the exotic has arrived at our neighborhood, and the cinemas of the world are waiting at our fingertips. Although I believe that the methodology for cultural exegesis proposed in this book can be applied to films of all cultures, its validity and reliability have been tested only with one case study. I am confident that the methodology can be customized to fit films of other cultures, which I hope will be confirmed by future research involving more case studies from other cinemas of the world.

1

———

Seeing the Unseen

Film as a Religious Experience

Seeing is not natural, however much we might think it to be.
  —Marcus Banks, visual anthropologist

The task I'm trying to achieve is, above all, to make you see.
  —D. W. Griffith, filmmaker

It was the summer of 1987. A group of rambunctious teenage boys in a conservative village in rural India decided to skip school, hop on a bus, and travel 20 miles east to the big city of Cochin. The boys were on a covert operation with one simple mission in mind: to watch a foreign film. An English flick, they were convinced, would deliver the enticing concoction of sex, drugs, and special effects that pushed far beyond the Bollywood boundaries.

To the boys' dismay, the only foreign film showing that day was from the equally conservative country of Japan. They were disappointed, but then they noticed the movie poster. It showed a seminude woman, pinned under a naked man with his hands cupping her breast. Another poster showed a woman shamelessly spreading her legs across the face of a man who appeared to be gaping into her groin. The boys silently agreed this was the film they would watch. They looked around and slowly snuck into the theater.

It only took a few minutes for the boys to realize that they had been taken for a ride. The film was about a primitive tribe in Japan. The suggestive posters were part of the tribe's attire. The alluded sex scenes were nothing but sporadic depictions of their tribal lifestyle. For the boys, the only good thing that came out of the experience was the fresh cold air of the air conditioner blowing in their jaded faces.

Within a few scenes, everyone was asleep. All except one—me. I could not sleep. The visuals were too captivating for me to look away. The scenes pulled me right into the middle of the exotic world that unfolded on the screen. Each frame had an emotional tone that resonated with the inherent connection between the animal world, the human world, and nature. The tribal life of the characters, often blurring the line between humans and beasts, made me laugh and cry simultaneously. This tribe was so distant yet so close; its people were right in front of me. Their world was strange yet familiar. Before I realized it, I had lost myself in their story. The film was a virtual vehicle into its diegetic world. For me, the film was a transcendent experience.

Little did I know that I was watching the masterpiece of a legendary filmmaker—Shohei Imamura, the only Japanese director to win the prestigious Palme d'Or prize at the Cannes Film Festival two times. The film I saw was *The Ballad of Narayama* (*Narayama-bushi kô*; 1983), now considered a modern classic by critics around the world.

The film tells the story of a tribal community in a remote Japanese island that exists under constant threat of famine and food deprivation. The villagers devise a strange custom to ensure their survival: everyone who turns seventy embraces voluntary death to make room for the next generation. This morbid custom is performed much like a sacred ritual. The elderly candidates leave their home on their seventieth birthday to climb the sacred mountains of Narayama, where they eventually starve themselves to death. The villagers understand life as a journey to the sacred mountains. The climb of Narayama is allegorical to a soul's ultimate ascent to its place of belonging.

The protagonist of the film is a family matriarch, Orin, who has just turned sixty-nine. The story revolves around her preparation for the sacred suicide. She sets the family affairs in order by arranging the marriage of her widower son, Tatsuhei, and disclosing the secret trout-fishing spot to her daughter-in-law, Tama. She even finds a temporary sexual partner for Risuke, whom all women in the village find repulsive.

The ritual is an act of sacrifice, but not all candidates are as calm and consenting as Orin. Tatsuhei's neighbor, for instance, must tie his father's arms and legs and drag him to his death, mercilessly ignoring his cry to live. Orin's family is prepared to renounce the tradition to save her life, but her determination is unflinching. In the emotionally charged climax, a reluctant Tatsuhei carries Orin on his back and leads her on the fateful trek.

Suddenly, the snow begins to fall. As Orin staggers through the slippery trails of Narayama, we almost feel the biting cold of death. She is grateful for this unexpected outpouring of snow, because it ensures a faster death by freezing in lieu of starvation. In the end, out of the blinding mist hovering over the mountains, Orin's smiling face emerges. In Imamura's visual poetry, death suddenly becomes a graceful event of beauty and elegance.

Seeing *The Ballad of Narayama* was, as far as I can remember, my first introduction to "world cinema." It was also the day I realized film's unmitigated power to transcend time and space and serve as a virtual portal into an unknown world. Watching this film was nothing less than a profound spiritual experience. The emotive power of the story instantly connected me to the life of "the other" and inspired a longing deep within me to rediscover the story of my own life.

Film as a Religious Encounter

Growing up in India, I was accustomed to the idiosyncratic relationship Indian viewers have with cinema. Unlike Western audiences, who tend to watch films in contemplative silence, the viewers in India are inclined to respond emotionally, instantly, and spontaneously to the film. The viewers in India tend to interact with the filmic world through a vicarious identification with the actors, often by singing and dancing along or whistling or booing at the actors. It is quite common to see the audience shouting or screaming at the screen when the plight of the protagonist seems to go awry. This interactive nature of film viewership makes it a participatory experience, enabling the audience to engage with the boisterous world projected on the screen.[1]

Film is an ordinary people's art form. It tells the stories of their life—triumphs, tragedies, and everything in between. Like religion,

---

1. "It would appear that the spectator subject of the Hindi cinema is positioned rather differently from that of much western cinema. In fact, even [at] the most overt level, Indian cinema audience behavior is distinctive: involvement in the film is intense, and audience [sic] clap, sing, recite familiar dialogue with the actors, throw coins at the screen (in appreciation of the spectacle) 'tut-tut' at emotionally moving scenes, cry openly and laugh and jeer knowingly" (Thomas 1985: 116).

film teaches us to respond to various life events and shows how to attribute meaning to these experiences. "Movies function as a primary source of power and meaning for people throughout the world," argues film professor Robert Johnston. "Along with the church, the synagogue, the mosque and the temple, they often provide people stories through which they can understand their lives" (2006: 13).

Of course, there are some films that portray stereotypical characters performing clichéd (im)moral tales. But today film has become a soul-searching medium, shaping the religious ethos of our postmodern mind. The infinite chasm between "secular" and "sacred" has collapsed in our world, allowing religion to reposition itself and reemerge in new shapes and forms—a process Christopher Deacy describes as "religious mutation" (2005: 27). While institutional religion is declining on a steep curve, "spirituality" is climbing up the same curve, becoming a compelling sociocultural phenomenon. "It is not the case that religion is fading with the secularization of society," say Martin and Ostwalt. "Rather religion is being popularized, scattered and secularized through extra-ecclesiastical institutions. We find ourselves in a contradictory age in which secularity and religious images coexist" (Martin and Ostwalt 1995: 157).

Also, the very act of going to the movies has become much like a religious ritual in our society today. Christopher Deacy observes, "In a matter analogous to traditional institutions such as the church, groups of people file into a theater at a specified time, choose a seat, and prepare with others for what could be said to amount to a religious experience" (2001: 4). Plate also notes how film viewing becomes "a social activity that alerts our interactions in the world. . . . Even if viewers do not know the people next to them in the movie house, their outlooks on the world, and thus also their social interactions, have been changed because of the film they have seen" (2003: 5). It is this opportunity to partake in a shared experience that brings people together into a movie theater and worship hall irrespective of their age, education, or social status. This is perhaps why we still patronize theaters even though movies are readily available from the comfort of our homes.

It is also believed that film creates "a cinematic experience that is said to be felt long before it is understood" (Deacy and Ortiz 2008: 201). The success of a film depends on viewers' identification with characters. As we see a reflection of our own selves in the characters of a film, we participate in their lives and even reinvent our own life story.

Therefore, a good film has transitive meanings, which can take the viewers beyond what it has intended, enabling them to discover their own meanings.

Film, like religion, functions as a narrative of culture. "Religion is (among other things) a narrative-producing mechanism," argues Melanie Wright. "And in this respect can be likened to both literature and the cinema" (2007: 4). In the same vein, Andrew Greeley also notes, "Religion is story before it is anything else and after it is everything else, as hope-renewing experiences are captured in symbols and woven into stories that are told and retold" (Bergesen and Greeley 2000: 15). Humanity has always engaged in storytelling. We make sense of the world around us in the form of stories. We write biography to share our own personal story, history to narrate the story of our society, and mythology to describe the story of the cosmos. Religion finds resonance with these cosmic narratives that we often call "myths."

A myth is essentially a story that "functions symbolically for a community to provide it with meaning and identity," and therefore "even films, can function as myths" (Lyden 2008: 212). Religion and film have similar goals in the sense that "both endeavor to make manifest the otherwise unpresentable" (Wright 2007: x). Just as religion creates mythologies to verbalize abstract truths, film creates "live myths" to visualize the intangible expressions that embody the norms and values that shape our culture. According to John Lyden, "The success or failure of a film largely correlates with whether it connects with viewers, that is, whether it is a 'live' myth that can speak to the worldview and values of a particular audience. In this way films can operate like religions for them" (2008: 217).

Film ensures not only the continuation of older myths but also the creation of new ones. The religious significance of film, according to Plate, lies in the fact that it has the power to change "the beliefs and practices, the myths and rituals, the symbolism and structures, of religion" (2003: 8). This change takes place through a "world-making process," which uses time and space as raw materials to build bridges between the world "out there" and the world "in here." We can see how film finds religious resonance in popular culture by participating in this myth-making process through film series such as Matrix trilogy (Neo, "the One," who escapes from the virtual prison created by artificial intelligence and comes back to save the rest of the world) and the Star Wars franchise (Luke Skywalker's journey in search of his identity guided by the "force").

In this way, according to Bryant, "movies do what we have always asked of popular religion, namely that they provide us with archetypical forms of humanity—heroic figures—and instruct us in the basic values and myths of our society" (Bryant 1982: 106). The heroic figure of a myth is on a journey, which dramatizes the conflicts we all face in life: choosing the right over the wrong. The hero teaches us how we should act when adversity strikes in the course of our lives, much in the same way we look up to heroes in television and film, hoping that their journey will help us overcome the obstacles we face in our own life journey toward purpose and meaning. The journey of the hero may be depicted on the screen as an adventurous trip to outer space, but in reality, it reflects our own journey to self-discovery.

Francis Cho, for example, talks about how certain films address the religious phenomena of attention and contemplation by imparting "a non-cognitive way of seeing" (2003: 78). The stylistic innovation of filmmakers such as Terrence Malik in *Tree of Life* (2001) and Bae Yong-kyun in *Why Has Bodhi Dharma Left for the East?* (1989) makes each of their films a visual meditation, where the viewers are invited to live in the "present" of their characters. Francis Cho considers this to be "a real-time experience, in which the camera holds our attention on an object for a duration of its (rather than our) choosing." (2003: 118). These types of films act as meditative and contemplative channels that expose the deep-rooted longings hidden in the dark recesses of our subconscious. Consider the following testimonial from experimental filmmaker Nathaniel Dorsky:

> I began to notice that moments of revelation or aliveness came to me from the way a filmmaker used film itself. Shifts of light from shot to shot, for instance, could be very visceral and effective. I began to observe that there was a concordance between film and our human metabolism, and to see that this concordance was fertile ground for expression. . . . I felt that the film itself had the potential to be transformative, to be an evocation of spirit, and to become a form of devotion. (Bandy and Monda 2003: 261)

Such esoteric encounters are also reflected in the theologian Paul Tillich. Tillich's autobiographical account of a serendipitous encounter he had with Sandro Botticelli's *Madonna with Singing Angels* is often used as an illustration of the revelatory nature of (fine) art.[2] He described

---

2. "Gazing up at it, I felt a state approaching ecstasy. In the beauty of the painting there was Beauty itself," Tillich wrote. "As I stood there, bathed in the beauty its painter had envisioned so long ago, something of the divine source of all things came through to me. I turned away shaken" (Tillich 1987: 234).

this experience as a "revelation in the language of religion." "That moment has affected my whole life," says Tillich, "giving me the keys for the interpretation of human existence, brought vital joy and spiritual truth" (1987: xix). As Paul Tillich suggests, "the experience is cultural in form and religious in substance. . . . It is cultural because it is not attached to a specific ritual act, but it is religious because it touches on the question of the Absolute and the limits of human existence" (2011: 68).

As in the opening story about the teenage boys in India, a film's ability to provide the viewers an experience of transcendence induces spiritual experiences in viewers' mind. In Johnston's view, the religious experience created by film is better understood in terms of transcendence—its ability to transport the viewers beyond themselves into authentic human condition or into the holy other. Johnston further argues that film has the power to provide the viewer with an experience of transcendence into authentic human condition (which he calls appropriation) or into the holy other (which he calls divine encounter). As Ken Gire notes, "What they [movies] do on a fairly consistent basis is give you an experience of transcendence. They let you lose yourself in somebody else's story" (1996: 120). Film, just like religion, can take a person beyond oneself in time and space and create "a sense of transcendence by pointing beyond the austerity and barrenness of the everyday world toward a higher, transcendent reality" (Deacy and Ortiz 2008, 43). Paul Schrader explores a specific style in certain films, which induces an experience of transcendence by gradually replacing the "abundant" cinematic means, which maintains viewer's voyeuristic interest, with "sparse" means, ultimately elevating the viewer's soul. Schrader analyzes the cinematic style of Yasujirô Ozu (1903–1963), Robert Bresson (1901–1999), and Carl Dryer (1889–1968) to observe how the monotony of the everyday world in their films signals to a transcendent reality capable of representing the invisible, the holy.[3] This transcendental style portrays "that invisible image in

3. Schrader (1988) proposes a fourfold step toward depicting transcendence in film. At first the film portrays "every day" in its coldness, with bland expressions and static composition. The notion of disparity constitutes the second step in transcendence, a potential disunity between man and his environment, which eventually culminates in a decisive action. What follows is a "decisive action," which is basically an incredible event happening within the banal reality of the everyday. It confronts the ineffable where the viewer realizes that there exists a transcendental realm of compassion to which man and nature reach out intermittently. The fourth and final stage is stasis, a static, quiescent, and organized scene, which underlines the newly derived idea of life at transcendence. The contradictory emotion is transformed to a unified and permanent expression in which man becomes one with nature again. Viewers accept this "irrationality" and thus transcend themselves to a "secondary reality."

which the parallel lines of religion and art meet and interpenetrate" (Schrader 1988: 169).

Religious Criticism of Film

Religious criticism of film strives to understand the subtle role religion plays in a film's meaning-making process. Film provides religious encounters for the postmodern mind. It reflects the ways in which we connect with transcendent realities outside the material realm. A film's interpretation of the religious dynamics of its context therefore plays a significant role in unpacking its meaning.

Film also provides insights into the dominant concerns in the society that religion needs to address. In other words, it is a way of watching a film with a lens crafted by the interpretive framework of religion. Film gradually moves from being an entertainment medium to becoming an exploratory medium, ideally serving both functions at the same time.

Gregory Watkins (2008) identifies four ways in which film becomes helpful in religious studies: First, film can communicate theological frameworks for understanding our religious experiences. Second, religious theories can be used to understand the meaning of a film. Third, film serves as "a window to another culture." And finally, film itself becomes a religious experience with its own sacramental qualities.

The methodology for cultural exegesis explained in chapter 4 focuses primarily on the third approach in Watkins's list, where film provides insights into the religious subsystem of its cultural matrix. Theological criticism falls into the remaining three categories in the list, depending on the approach adopted by the critic. This book provides a particular emphasis on the dialogical approach, where the theological framework for unpacking the meaning of the film will be borrowed from the film itself.

Martin and Ostwalt's (1995) *Screening the Sacred* classified the religious criticism of film in three basic categories: (1) theological criticism, which interprets the film in the context of traditional religious and theological categories; (2) mythological criticism, which illustrates the religious functioning of film in terms of universal archetypes; and (3) ideological criticism, which unpacks the meaning of film in relation to sociocultural ideologies.

Critiquing film from the perspective of religion involves a complex process riddled with many theoretical and methodological hurdles. There is an inherent skepticism in academia toward the discipline, because most critics in the field are Christian theologians with an overt agenda. Malory Nye voices this concern as she observes, "It seems that the majority of those working in cultural studies have yet to be convinced that religious studies scholars are not closet theologians" (2003: 17). Wright criticizes the "theologically driven instrumentalism" of the critics, which denigrates the film to an instrument to project theological themes of a particular faith tradition. She argues their selection of films is inconsistent, the interpretation is solipsistic, and the criticism is "confined to their own personal musings."[4] Others, such as David Jasper, Brent Plate, and Steve Nolan, seem to agree with Wright while also accusing them of focusing too much on narrative and literary methods, leaving hardly any room for interdisciplinary dialogues.

This criticism seems to be valid prima facie, since the scholars who dominate the field of religious criticism of film are predominantly Western theologians. The interpretive lens immediately available to them is shaped by Judeo-Christian theology. However, it should be remembered that the films they usually work with are from Hollywood or Europe, where the underlying worldview assumptions are also shaped by the same theology. Therefore, as Sheila Nayar suggests, "we should not be too hasty . . . in interpreting this as a signal of imperialistic drives or of the analysts' inherent discriminatory nature" (2012: 36). The so-called theological baggage works to their advantage and contributes to the process of unpacking the meaning of each film.

What if we consider theology itself as another method in religious criticism of film? Even Wright, who is a strong critic of theologians, admits that any theological assumptions of the critic should not be "the starting point of theory, but . . . must not be neglected" (2007: 12). All critics have their own closet ideologies, be they theistic, nontheistic, or atheistic. In that sense, a critic's "theological baggage" is an inevitable hurdle, which can only be overcome by incorporating corrective measures into the methodology. In traditional film criticism, a movie is understood based on a specific interpretive framework, such as the author's intentions (auteur criticism), text of the movie (narrative criticism), or ideological context (feminist, Marxian, postcolonial, queer theory, etc.). In the same way, religious criticism as a theological approach can function as a critical framework with its own specific methodologies.

---

4. As observed by Jonathan Brant (2012: 22).

What Does Theology Have to Do with Religion?

Religious scholarship has a spectrum of vantage points. An anthropologist, for instance, might consider religion a cultural category, while a theologian might consider religion a revelation of a supranatural agent. The former is a functional approach to religion, which categorizes it as a cultural phenomenon that influences social norms, values, and worldview assumptions. The latter focuses on the substantive aspect, dealing with the belief systems and doctrinal assertions of religion.

Broadly speaking, academia in the Western world is confined to the parameters of the naturalistic precepts of the social sciences, which has no categories to conceptualize the supranatural manifestation of religion. It tries to understand religion merely from a functional perspective—perhaps the psychological experiences of individuals or cultural expressions of a community. It assumes that any substantive truth about religion is shaped entirely by cultural evolution. There are no absolute truths against which religious experiences can be evaluated or validated.

This is a biased assumption, of course, albeit a necessary one, if one needs to indulge the naturalistic precepts of scientific methodologies. However, in reality, we find ourselves living in a world where the opposite is equally true. In a post-9/11 world, truth-claims of religious groups dictate cultural behavior, challenge social structures, and even threaten social order. We witness the substantive assertions of religion shaping its cultural manifestation as much as they are also being shaped in the process of cultural evolution.

As a whole, we must come to terms with the fact that the ethical and moral codes devised by people are integrally connected to their substantive understanding of religion (or lack thereof). A person's perception of the cosmos and supranatural realities influences social values and behaviors. For example, belief in reincarnation is a substantive proposition based on the sacred texts of Hinduism, according to which human beings are caught in a cycle of births and rebirths controlled by their actions or karma. Since Hinduism is the dominant religion in India, this dogma affects the social and cultural landscapes. In the same way, many political issues that polarize the Western world today derive from the substantive claims of Judaism and Christianity.

Every religion claims to have its own established a priori theological assumptions, and determining these assumptions is crucial to understanding any religion. Theology deals with the substantive truths of religion and defines the cosmic relationships between human beings and transcendent entities, often in the form of personal devotion to God (or gods). Theology influences culture as much as culture influences theology. Therefore, this symbiotic relationship between theology and culture can be represented as a transactional process; figure 1.1 illustrates the relationship between the functional and substantive dimensions of religion.

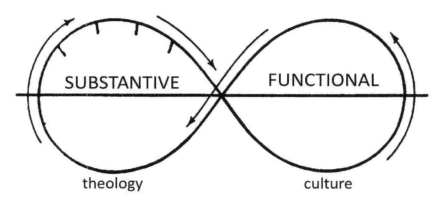

SUBSTANTIVE   FUNCTIONAL

theology   culture

Fig. 1.1. *Functional and Substantive Dimensions of Religion*

This symbiotic figure is a dynamic system of interdependence where substantive and functional dimensions of religion both borrow from and contribute to each other through an incessant transactional process. Both theological and cultural rhetoric feed into each other through this oscillatory process.

The system loses its balance, however, when one side of the cycle overtakes the other. In a religiously conservative society, theology dominates culture. In a secularized society, in contrast, culture overpowers and shapes theology.

A religious critic of film, therefore, should wear spectacles with a theological lens on one eye and a cultural lens on the other (see table 1.1). Theological criticism will look at film "from above," observing the transcendental meanings embedded within it, while a cultural exegesis of the film will look at it "from below," paying attention to the cultural perceptions of religion within its diegetic world. An interlacing of both methodologies establishes a more holistic interpretation of the religious in film. Experience of the transcendent invoked by the film draws attention to theological themes, while the human response to the transcendent sheds light on cultural themes.

Table 1.1

Two Lenses for Religious Interpretation of Film

Theological Lens	Cultural Lens
God is central to film criticism.	Humanity/culture is the focus of the criticism.
Film itself can become a religious experience.	Film is an instrument for observing religious experience or religious phenomenology.
What is God saying to us through the film?	How does culture perceive the supernatural?
Focus is on what God reveals to humanity.	Focus is on human search for the supernatural.
Downward direction: from God to human	Upward direction: from human to cosmos
The Spirit of God reveals eternal truths.	The human spirit explores the meaning of life.
Realm of thoughts	Realm of practices: myth, ritual, folklore, etc.

Theologies of religions may be otherworldly for academia, but they have significant consequences in shaping our worldviews and social behavior. Any attempt to consider religion merely as a social system (the functional dimension of religion) with no reference to its theology (the substantive dimension of religion) is nothing but a mockery of the discipline itself. An integration of the functional aspects of religion emerging from the exegetical process, and the substantive aspect of religion discovered through theological criticism, will facilitate a religious reading of the film. Therefore, in religious criticism of film, we perform methodologies from both fields in tandem, exploring God's revelation to culture as well as the cultural perception of God.

Summary

Film has grown into an authentic mode of self-expression in our post-modern world, delving deeper into human condition its abstract experiences. The recent shift in film production from studio to indie projects has accoutered filmmakers with the capacity to deal with themes that are closer to their heart, with little interference from outside agencies. As more and more films are setting out to explore existential themes and transcendent realities, film is becoming a "naked portrait of human essence" that reflects "our quest for human meaning and fulfillment" (Deacy and Ortiz 2008).

Religion is both a cultural enterprise performed by humans and a revelatory expression initiated by God. A critic should therefore combine both cultural and theological methods and consider religion an "interplay between revelation of the transcendent and the response of the human" (Turner 1981: 35). A separation between the functional and the substantive is virtually impossible in most parts of the world, where cultural phenomena are filtered through a theological lens. Both the cultural perceptions of God (religion) and God's revelation to culture (theology) in a given context can thus be explored through films.

2

Theological Criticism of Film

A Substantive Lens on Religion

There is a story about the Greek gods.
They were bored, so they invented human beings.
But they were still bored. So they invented love.
Then they weren't bored any longer.
  So they decided to try love for themselves.
  —*Feast of Love* (2007)

Morgan Freeman's character in *Feast of Love* talks about the deep longing gods possess to be part of the human story. They descend from Mount Olympus in the west or Mount Kailas in the east and walk among us to experience the pleasures of our carnal life. The sages who come face-to-face with these lovesick gods capture their passion and call it divine revelation. The esoteric stories they write about these encounters become sacred scriptures, giving birth to religions around the world.

Of course, this is nothing but a fanciful story for academics. We, instead, are preoccupied with the naturalistic assumptions of the material sciences against any intangible realities in human experience. But the fact remains, it is implausible to understand religion without first understanding the fragments of divine revelation each culture claims to have received in their timeless past. Theological criticism focuses precisely on this "forbidden" zone—the role of supranatural categories in the meaning-making process of a film.

A Foundational Framework for Theological Criticism of Film

The underlying assumption in theological criticism is that film is a medium of divine revelation, filtered through the narrative sensibilities of the filmmakers and the filmmaking context. By delving deeper into the theological center of the narrative, we get to explore the substantive elements of religion represented in film. Criticism thus looks at how a culture defines the relationship between nomos and cosmos, which is integral to the religious reading of film.

In the initial stages of its development, religious criticism of film employed Paul Tillich's theology of culture as a foundational framework. In Tillich's approach, the critic was driven by the belief that film was a medium of God's general revelation manifested in the artistic self-expression of the auteur.[1] Over time, the attention shifted from the filmmaker to the film itself, where the study of cinematic language became an important criterion for theological analysis. Contemporary religious critics have shown an increasing commitment to film theories, culture theories, and reception theories (Plate 2003).

The very first attempt to analyze film from a theological perspective is believed to be an essay "The Religious Possibilities of Motion Picture," written by Herbert Jump in 1911. Jump used the parables of Jesus as an interpretive framework to look at the film text. Neil Hurley's *Theology through Film* (1970) was perhaps the pioneer attempt to provide a methodology for critiquing film from a theological standpoint. As film communicates universal human needs, Hurley believed, film also created an experience that touches the nerves that "reach into the core of our lives." These visual experiences created by film contain our past, reflect our present, and project our future. The imageries

---

1. Even today, many critics find Tillich's model a useful device in creating a framework for critiquing films from a theological standpoint. Jonathan Brant recently conducted empirical research to the test the model through audience response analysis (Brant 2012). Developing a survey with qualitative questions that might suggest revelatory experiences, Brant identified a group of people who claim to have had mystical experiences while watching films. These individuals were then introduced to Tillich's life, thought, and theology of revelation to see if they had a similar experience while watching the film. This qualitative research concludes that the mystical encounter they experienced was not predicated upon the explicit religious content of the film. Rather, a deep connection the viewer felt through something in the film that resonated with his or her own personal life generated a religious experience in the viewer's mind.

emerging from the film shape a "transcendental ethic, maturing with the strength of humanity's growing awareness," which is theological in its root.

In the 1990s, Larry Kreitzer in the United Kingdom (*The New Testament in Fiction and Film: On Reversing the Hermeneutic Flow*) and Robert Jewett in the United States (*St. Paul at the Movies: The Apostle's Dialogue with American Culture*) applied hermeneutic principles from the field of biblical studies to understand the meaning of film. Albert Bergesen and Andrew M. Greeley's *God in the Movies* (2000) offered a social-science angle to theological criticism, while Margaret Miles pioneered the application of culture studies methodology in religion and film dialogue. In her *Seeing and Believing: Religion and Values* (1996), Miles used her background in historical theology to analyze the social and political context of film production and showed how they deal with crucial cultural questions such as race, gender, sexuality, and morality. According to Miles, film is not a substitute but a preparation for religion with a potential to reform the society by pointing its audience to a particular direction, even if it does not occupy a moral position.

John Lyden (2003) raised the stakes by suggesting that film not only reflects the religious sentiments, but also functions as religion itself, with its own sacramental qualities. While Marsh and Deacy believed that audience recreates the film narrative using its own theological assumptions to discover new meanings, Lyden insisted that the viewers do not always impose their reading on film; rather, they receive its meaning unconsciously. According to Johnston, "Movies can and do perform religious functions in culture today as they communicate a society myth, ritual and symbol and provide a web of fundamental belief" (Johnston 2006: 73). Brent Plate (2008) corroborated this argument by explaining how film invents a mythical world through techniques such as framing and projecting. Both Lyden and Plate explained how films participate in a mythmaking process by showing how myths and rituals influence the way films are made and interpreted.

Clive Marsh and Gaye Ortiz's *Explorations in Theology and Film* (1997) proposed systematic theology, ranging from Christology to eschatology, as an interpretive framework for religious criticism. Christopher Deacy suggested Richard Niebuhr's Christ-culture paradigm as a model for theological criticism. The message of a film is always antithetical to theology in the "Christ against culture" model, whereas the film is theologized to attribute unwarranted meanings in the "Christ of culture" model. A critic should avoid these extreme positions and follow "the dualist, synthetic and conversionist models," where "film can clearly contribute to Christian theology although Christian theology brings its own agenda to the conversation" (Deacy and Ortiz 2008: 67). In a synthetic paradigm ("Christ is above culture"), theological criticism becomes an exploration of human experiences, searching for the glimpses of the divine that point to the "wholly other." In a dualist paradigm ("Christ and culture in paradox"), it takes place in the form of dialogue, focusing more on the divergent themes between religion and film than on the convergent themes. In the conversionist paradigm ("Christ is the transformer of the culture"), theological criticism focuses on convergent themes such as grace and redemption, available both in religion and film because Christ transforms the fallenness of humanity and the depravity of culture through a conversion experience.

Johnston used a similar framework to map the dialectic stance between theology and film. The initial stance of theology is avoidance, where film has nothing to contribute to theology. Theological criticism becomes a moral judgment on film from an opposing platform. In the next stance, theology is willing to learn from film, but the process of learning has to be done with caution. The third stance, dialogue, invites both theology and film to enter into a conversation as equal partners where the critics "first view a film on its own terms before entering into theological dialogue with it." In the fourth stance, appropriation, theology appreciates film's vision of life and appropriates religious experiences out of human experiences. In the fifth stance, Johnston contemplates the possibility of film becoming a medium for divine encounter by revealing God's presence more sharply and effectively, providing the viewer an experience of transcendence in to the Holy Other.[2] Theological criticism takes place within this continuum between avoidance and divine encounter, depending on the position a critic assumes along the spectrum (Johnston 2000). The gradual evolution of the framework for theological criticism can be described in the form of a flow chart (see fig. 2.1).

Let us now look at three methodological approaches prevalent in the field of theological criticism of film before I propose my own methodology for religious reading of film.

---

2. To illustrate this point, Johnston uses his own example of hearing a calling to ministry as he was watching Beckett.

An Instrumental Approach:
Interpretation of Religious Films

We have witnessed in recent years the flourishing of the so-called faith-based market in Hollywood. Most faith-based films are cliché-driven morality tales with predictable plots and melodramatic religious encounters. As much as these films appeal to niche audiences, they also alienate other viewers, fostering a cancerous growth of isolated religious subcultures in our society.

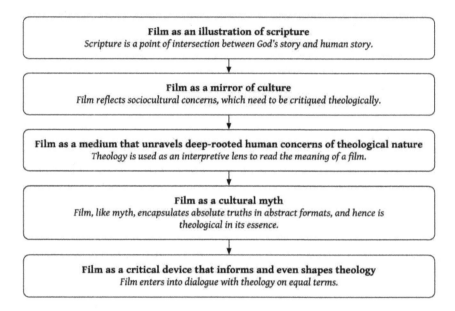

Fig. 2.1. *Evolution of Theological Criticism of Film*

This is an instrumental approach to film, where film is perceived merely as an instrument to convey a theological agenda. It comes loaded with its own interpretive framework, leaving little room for critical engagement. The film answers the questions raised by itself, and the theological meaning of the film is clearly stated in the narrative.

Of course, religious institutions have the right to make films for educational or promotional purpose to survive in a society obsessed with visual media. However, the denigration of film merely to the level of a teaching tool undermines its potential to create meaningful experiences for the viewers. The religious value of film resides not in its ability to convey religious ideas, but in its ability to create theological experiences. Only when the stimulus of a film transcends our cognitive level and enters into the affective core can it become a catalyst for radical transformation of the self.

An Illustrative Approach:
Theological Interpretation of Film

In the illustrative approach, a film becomes an illustration of the theological worldview subscribed by the critic. The critic attempts to provide theological explanations to the events depicted in the filmic word, using the truth that religion already possesses. Film is not a source material for drawing theology; instead, theology contributes to the meaning of the film.

The meaning of a film is transitive, not inherent. Like any other forms of story, a film narrative is also open to interpretation. Great films have multiple levels of meaning, and they let viewers create their own meanings, apart from what is intended by the auteur. When film is interpreted from a theological viewpoint, new meanings emerge, and therefore the task of the critic is to discern these hidden meanings embedded in the film. Theological themes can be found even in films that do not have explicit religious content. The focus of the criticism, therefore, is not on the religious content of the film itself, but on its power to evoke religious sentiments in the viewers' mind.

The illustrative methodology is susceptible to the danger of biased interpretation, where critics find whatever they are looking for in the film. Critics determine meanings by attribution, forcing viewers to read a film based on their theological presuppositions. It may not be motivated purely by self-interest, as in the case of the instrumental approach, but the inevitable absence of dialogue makes it more of a pragmatic methodology than a critical one.

Film is used mostly as a resource from which we can draw theological themes that match our worldview assumptions. One such theme is the so-called Christ figures that dominated the field of theological criticism in the early stage of its development (see appendix 2). According to the proponents of this theory, certain films contain symbolic figures called Christ figures, which exhibit the fundamental nature of Christ's redemptive work. Critics assume that Christ is present in the film "in cognito" (Marsh 2004: 51) and attribute the redemptive features of Christ into one of the characters in the film. This method has been widely criticized by scholars, yet it provides interesting insights into the many ways a film resonate with religious sentiments of the critic.

An Interactive Approach:
Film and Theology in Dialogue

In the interactive mode, core values reflected in the film are brought into conversation with core assumptions of theology. It insists on a "film qua film" approach, where a film needs to be critiqued on its own terms. Instead of interpreting films using preconceived theological theories, we bring theology and film into a dialogue, where the film is allowed to critique and even inform theology as much as it is critiqued and informed by theology. Within the interactive approach, a film is neither an instrument for conveying religious ideas nor an illustration of preconceived theological theories, but rather a resource from which we can learn and derive new theology.

The interactive approach explores the theology of the film instead of imposing a critic's theology on film. "Theologizing should follow," argues Johnston, "not precede, the aesthetic experience" (2006: 64). It is important to listen carefully to what the film is trying to communicate before entering into interpretive process. "Personal evaluation, including theological dialogue, has its place as in any human encounter," says Johnston. "But it must follow the act of first looking and listening" (2006: 239). Once the film is analyzed using traditional methodologies of film analysis, we wait for theological themes to emerge from its narrative core.

The key emphasis here is on an attitude of humility, where criticism begins from the works of filmmakers, not from the works of theologians. Filmmakers and theologians are equal partners in dialogue. Filmmakers need not be "religious" for their film to be considered for theological analysis. "Does it matter whether Shakespeare believed in witches?" asks a critic (Bergesen and Greeley 2000, 141). According to Saint Paul, seeking minds meet the revealing Spirit of God even if it is as if "looking through a glass darkly" (1 Cor 13:12). Therefore, "films do not have to have obvious religious content in order to function religiously in either an individual or a corporate manner" (Ostwalt 2008: 35).

To initiate a proper dialogue, we need to understand that theology, like film, is also an abstract art, not an absolute science. We need to set aside the dogmatic assertions of propositional truths and accept religion as the "story" that describes the human journey in search of meaning. All artistic explorations of human nature have the potential to provide theological insights. Therefore, "film can (and should) challenge our reading of theology just as theology can (and should) challenge our reading of films" (Deacy and Ortiz 2008: 209).

A Methodology for Theological Criticism

In deriving a methodology for theological criticism, we consider film, first and foremost, as a storytelling medium. The story told through film creates a cinematic experience through a fusion of sound (music), images, and text, in a manner no other medium can replicate (see fig. 2.2). As Deacy notes, "Cinematic fiction, with its gift of image, narrative and sound, can tell a story like no other human art form yet invented" (Deacy and Ortiz 2008: 209).

Johnston believes that story lies at the theological center of the film. Good theology, like good film, emerges from a good story. In a typical film narrative, the protagonist embarks on a journey in search of redemption, where he or she is confronted with a conflict. The transformation that happens to the characters as they handle the conflict is expressed as the character arc. Theological themes emerge from the ethical concerns the characters face as they deal with the conflict or the blissful event of redemption they experience in the process. The character arc often includes grace events that cannot always be explained by human reason. These events oftentimes communicate spiritual experiences better than any contrived religious symbol.

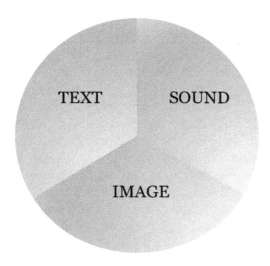

Fig. 2.2. *Film as Story*

Religion, after all, is the grand story of redemption. Its main promise to humanity is hope. As Detweiler suggests, despite all the evidence that suggests life as fallen, confused, and bleak, we still cling to hope in an eternal future. The events of redemption and the promise of hope in a film almost always direct us to a realm beyond our reason, where it becomes *locus theologicus*—a place for divine revelation (Detweiler 2007: 256). As Johnston suggests, film provides experiences of transcendence into authentic human condition through appropriation, or into the "holy other," through divine encounter. The experience may not necessarily be religious, but there is a religious dimension to the event. It may be illusory and temporal, yet it creates a sacred space in which viewers experience theophany and receive theological insights.

In Johnston's observation of appropriation, religious experiences are appropriated out of human experiences, creating a vision of life that extends the boundaries of our imaginative horizon. Anthony Sison extends this idea further to incorporate a "deep focus of humanity" he observes in certain films. This is particularly applicable to "third world cinema," where the idea of God "is sympathetic to and in solidarity with the third world struggle for decolonization and emancipation" (2012: 71). In an unjust world full of suffering, whatever inspires us to fight against injustice and ultimately overcome suffering is truly divine. Therefore, the depiction of human struggle against all forms of oppression provides religious experiences rooted in humanity.

us to fight against injustice and ultimately overcome suffering is truly divine. Therefore, the depiction of human struggle against all forms of oppression provides religious experiences rooted in humanity.

Since both religion and film tell stories of how people find meaning in their life, we conclude that all films, regardless of culture, to some extent possess "theological" threads. Religion and films alike grapple with some degree of existential issues, such as theodicy, guilt, or forgiveness, which are essentially theological in nature. Theological themes are therefore inherent in film.

The methodologies for theological criticism are characteristically different from the scientific conventions of traditional film criticism. This methodological process begins with a "film analysis," where the artistic structure of the film is dissected to reveal the true meaning of the story. Appendix 3 provides an approach to film analysis, primarily drawing from Johnston's (2000) methodology for narrative criticism and the Yale *Film Analysis Guide* (Prunes et al. 2002). Once we interpret film on its own terms, theological themes start emerging from the core of its visual narrative. These are some questions to guide theological criticism of film:

1. How is religion treated in the film? Is religion central to the plot or a backdrop to the main narrative?
2. How does the film differentiate between the secular and the sacred? What is the primary worldview in which the film operates?
3. Does the film depict any supranatural entities? Is there explicit or implicit portrayal of a God-figure?
4. Does the film refer to any sacred scriptures? If so, what role does scripture play in the narrative? Does the film do more than illustrate a truth that is already known from scripture? Does it uncover the meaning of scripture?
5. Where do the characters of the film derive meaning to their life? How does the film portray death? Does it deal directly with the question of life after death?
6. How do the characters react to conflict? Does their religious belief (or lack thereof) play a role in their decision-making process?
7. What are the moral/ethical/social values implied in the film? Do they have any religious connotations? Does the film complement or challenge these values?

8. What are the themes that emerge from the theological center of the film, such as grace, forgiveness, redemption, theodicy, freewill, or destiny?
9. Does the film move you emotionally, spiritually, or intellectually? How does the film touch your inner being?
10. Does the film induce a spiritual or transcendent experience for you? If so, how and why?

In the final analysis, theological criticism does not always have to go to theology, but it does always appeal to the evocative power of film. This power enables us to surface the experiences of the divine within human experiences. Even films with no explicit religious agenda can thus provide us with religion-like experiences and a meaningful dialogue between film and theology.

According to Jewish and Christian theology, human beings are created in the image and likeness of God. Authentic humanity, therefore, is a mirror reflection of divinity. As Bresson puts it, "If there is a human presence, there is a divine presence."[3] In that sense, true religious essence of the film rests in its ability to portray what is fully human. This is the heart of appropriation, which is a particularly useful concept in developing a methodology for world cinema, as it finds a common ground among the diverse theologies of world religions.

However, from a postmodern perspective, any attempt to claim a film qua film approach can be perceived as an intellectual deception. True interpretation can happen only through the self-awareness of critics and the disclosure of their theological biases. Therefore, "religious interpreters of film need to be more aware of, and consciously working from, the particular hermeneutical (including theological) traditions within which they stand" (Marsh 1998: 198).

Summary

Film stories, as Deacy puts it, "help in our quest for human meaning and fulfillment" (Deacy and Ortiz 2008: 203). The primary factor that invokes religious experience in a film is the implication of a higher purpose and meaning in its story. Although audiovisual elements are important, the story should remain the focal point in theological criticism. The experiences created by sensory elements are transitive, as their intended function is to draw the viewers into the story.

---

3. Dialogue from the film *Au Hazard Balthazar* (1966); quoted by Cunneen 2003: 108.

The dynamic language of film can communicate theological truths better than the static language of text. We would therefore adopt an interactive approach, which calls for film analysis using traditional methods of film criticism while also facilitating a reciprocal exchange between theology and film. The criticism begins from the theological point of view of the film before being filtered through the hermeneutical lens of the critic. The emphasis is on paying judicious respect to the messages that both film and theology are trying to communicate to one other, rather than one being used to serve the specific interest of the other.

The dialogical method proposed by Johnston serves as an ideal framework for critiquing films from a theological perspective. Johnston's students, including Craig Detweiler, Barry Taylor, and Kutter Callaway, have since extended this methodology and applied the process to various artifacts of popular culture. Drawing from the same source, my objective is to customize this methodology for world cinema by extending its boundaries beyond the culture-specific assumptions of Western film criticism.

3

Cultural Exegesis of Film

A Functional Lens on Religion

> Tiger got to hunt, bird got to fly;
> Man got to sit and wonder "why, why, why?"
> Tiger got to sleep, bird got to land;
> Man got to tell himself he understands.
> —Kurt Vonnegut, *Cat's Cradle*

In 1971, the University of Chicago accepted *Cat's Cradle*, a novel written by Kurt Vonnegut Jr., as a thesis submission towards his master of arts degree in anthropology. It was an unprecedented step in the academic world. *Cat's Cradle* was not scientific research; it was a work of fiction.[1] How, some questioned, can fiction qualify as rigorous academic work? Many are familiar with the adage "Truth is stranger than fiction." But this unprecedented step begs the question: is fiction as credible as truth?

Ethnographic research is perceived as an interpretive process rather than scientific analysis in the postmodern theoretical framework of cultural anthropology. Instead of searching for patterns across different cultures, a postmodern ethnographer creates "thick descriptions" of culture by interpreting the meaning of cultural symbols within a

---

1. *Cat's Cradle* narrates a fictional story with the atomic bombing of Hiroshima as a backdrop.

specific context and re-presenting them using literary methods.[2] The unique ability of film to integrate text, performance, and image into storytelling process makes it an exceptional platform for creating such thick descriptions. Therefore, narrative feature films can function as cultural documents, yielding valuable ethnographic data of its context—its production, distribution, and consumption.

Culture as Cinema

A film does something more than present a descriptive documentation of culture; film also recreates the emotional experiences associated with cultural events. It helps the viewers virtually experience a culture, which means they not only get to see a visual representation of culture, but also get an opportunity to "sense" it. In this way, film creates a participatory experience of culture, accentuated by story, performance, and image.

Since film is essentially a combination of fiction, performance, and image, we will explore three major ways in which culture is perceived in ethnographic research: culture as fiction, culture as performance, and culture as image (see fig. 3.1).

2. Geertz (1973) illustrated the concept of "thick description" using an example that I will reproduce here in my own words: There are four people in a room. The first person's eye is twitching rapidly because of a health condition. The second person's eye is also twitching, but he is winking his eyes to give a signal to someone else. The third person's eyelids are also in rapid motion, but he is neither twitching nor winking, but mimicking (parodying) the actions of the first two. The fourth person is also performing the same action, but he is actually "rehearsing," or learning how to wink as a signal to another person. According to Geertz, a "thin description" for describing everybody's action would be to say, "rapidly contracting eyelids." But that description gives the impression that the people are all doing the same thing. A thin description cannot illustrate the different meanings of the same action as it is performed by four people. Only a thick description can explain what each person is "actually" doing by interpreting the contextual meaning of each action. In other words, observation of facts in ethnographic research is not merely an objective phenomenon; it also involves a process of interpretation of the facts. Ethnography should then be able to elaborate these contextual meanings in the form of a thick description.

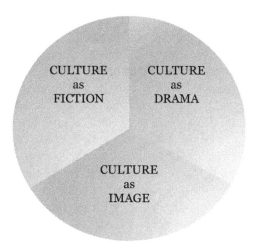

Fig. 3.1. *Culture as Cinema*

Postmodern theoreticians have created new possibilities in which ethnography is guided by the implicit narrative structure of a story. Interpretive anthropology, proposed by Clifford Geertz, permits creative modes of cultural representation, where ethnographic writing is considered a subjective "invention" or "fashioning" of observed events. All cultural representations are second- or third-order interpretations, and therefore, all ethnographies can be considered as "fictions, in the sense that they are 'something made,' or 'something fashioned'" (Geertz 1973: 15). He advocates for the power of "scientific imagination" in ethnography that brings the reader into a personal encounter with the subject. In the same vein, James Clifford also argues that, "ethnographic texts are . . . constructed domains of truth, serious fictions" (1988: 10). Ethnography can be deliberately discursive, presenting thick descriptions of culture in creative formats, including fictive narration.

Victor Turner described culture as drama, because, according to him, humans are performing animals or "*Homo performans.*" As William Shakespeare famously suggested, "All the world's a stage, and all the men and women merely players."[3] We try to discover our identity through reflexive cultural performances. All parts of cultural performance, including ritual, ceremony, carnival, theater, and poetry, are "explanation and explication of life itself" (Turner 1982: 13). Individ-

3. *As You Like It*, act 2, scene 7.

through reflexive cultural performances. All parts of cultural performance, including ritual, ceremony, carnival, theater, and poetry, are "explanation and explication of life itself" (Turner 1982: 13). Individuals interpret cultural contexts "in order to act" (Geertz 1973: 71) in a series of performances, which Turner describes as "social dramas" (Turner 1979: 62). Major genres of cultural performance (from ritual to theater) and narration (from myth to the novel) originate from and continue in the form of social dramas. Like a stage drama, social drama also has a plot structure that involves conflict and resolutions, involving interactions, transactions, and reciprocities. Turner's "anthropology of performance" and Schechner's (1990) "performance theory" connected social dramas to theater performances, which can be considered analogous to screen performances.

The emerging field of visual anthropology has initiated new paradigms for visualizing culture as image. Social scientists rarely use images as a means for communicating scientific thought, except for illustrative purposes. But visual anthropology employs image as a primary mode of communication, and the camera is a principal tool of ethnographic investigation. Image, however, is no more transparent than the text itself. A camera lets us see a cultural event, but to experience it, we need a thick description of its context. The camera is nothing but an extension of ethnographic gaze, and the image is still a thin description of culture. According to Marcus Banks, the true story of an image is told by a combination of both "internal narrative," which is the iconographic knowledge of the image itself, and "external narrative," which is ethnographic knowledge constructed by conducting research outside the image. Internal narrative deals with the form, asking, "What is the image of?" whereas external narratives construct the story of the image, asking contextual questions such as "Who took this picture?" "When was it taken?" and "Why was it taken?" The meaning of the image and meaning of the context are therefore "mutually constituting" (Banks 2007: 41).

The field of visual anthropology gave birth to ethnographic films. These films follow a scientific methodology to document culture using a specific theoretical lens. However, the fact remains that they suffer from the problem of subjectivity as much as fictional films do. After all, the presence of the ethnographer and the technology involved in the filming and editing processes significantly alter the perceived reality of events (see appendix 1). In the end, filmmakers and ethnographers share similar goals to record, interpret, and represent culture.

For ethnographers, film is a means to an end, but for filmmakers, film is an end in itself. Table 3.1 summarizes how Heider tabulates the differences between an ethnographer and a filmmaker (2006: 8).

Ethnographer	Filmmaker
Begins with a theoretical problem and plans the research	Begins with an idea and a script
Gathers data by making observations and asking questions	Shoots footage based on the script
Analyzes data, writes, and rewrites	Edits footage based on a point of view
Produces a written report (ethnography)	Produces a film

Table 3.1 *Ethnographer vs. Filmmaker*

We cannot disregard cinema as a "fictional" product simply because it does not fit into our traditional understanding of realism. Cinema is, of course, a subjective interpretation of reality, but according to the precepts of postmodern anthropology, it is precisely the same subjectivity that qualifies it as a credible cultural document. Ethnographic films, therefore, have the liberty to use fictional story lines and thoughtfully planned filming techniques to "manipulate reality through a series of falsehoods in order to create a higher truth" (Heider 2006: 10).

Another important component of film that is intentionally left out in this conversation is music. Film music in itself has the capacity to function as a datum of culture and warrants extensive analysis through the methodologies of ethnomusicology. For the purposes of the methodology for cultural exegesis of film, music would be considered one of the many factors that affect the performance aspect of the film narrative. Miguel Mera and Anna Morcom note that mediated music has the ability to "span contexts across time and space, transcending the boundaries of live performance" (2009: 6). Music adds vitality to performance by adding tone, rhythm, and mood to the drama, increasing its emotional impact. Whether it is ritual or theater, music enhances drama by connecting the audience vicariously to the diegetic world of the film. This is why Larsen compared film music to a hypnotist with "a direct link with the unconscious" (2005: 196).

Three elements can be combined to create a new theoretical framework for understanding culture as cinema: a *fictional story* is being *performed* to create *visual representations* of culture. We can, therefore, incorporate insights from interpretive anthropology, performance anthropology, and visual anthropology into traditional film criticism to create a new methodology for cultural exegesis of film, which provide a thicker description of a culture.

A Methodology for Cultural Exegesis of Film

The first step in reading religion from film through a functional lens is to extract the ethnographic information embedded within the film narrative. This process is referred to as cultural exegesis of film,[4] not to be confused with other methods in traditional film criticism, such as cultural criticism.

The key task of cultural criticism is to identify the positioning of a film within its specific sociocultural matrix. It explores the ways in which the film responds to various ideological concerns of its context and how it influences audience's understanding of social issues. All film-viewing experience has a cultural context. The meaning of film is not determined by the film itself, but through an interaction of "texts, spectators, institutions and the ambient culture" (Wright 2007: 26).

Cultural exegesis, in contrast, is the process of reading ethnographic information from a film, assuming it is a datum of culture. It looks at film as a field of research from which ethnographic data can be collected and analyzed using traditional methods of ethnographic research. We make ethnographic inquiry within the diegetic world of the film to understand the functional role religion plays in the society represented in the film.

In a nutshell, both cultural criticism and cultural exegesis explore the relationship between the world inside and outside of the film, but they look at film from diametrically different perspectives. Cultural criticism looks at culture to gain insights for interpreting the meaning of the film. Cultural exegesis looks at film to observe culture and interpret its meaning.

The exegesis starts with a process called virtual participant obser-

---

4. *Exegesis* is a term seldom referred to in ethnographic research, though it is frequently used in semantic discourses to describe the technical structure of a text. It is typically associated with hermeneutics, which interprets the meaning of the text in a given context by examining various presuppositions involved in the process of communication. Geertz used hermeneutics to understand the ways that people "understand and act in social, religious, and economic contexts," whereas Turner used it as a method for understanding the meanings of cultural performances such as dance and drama (Woodward 1996:12). Exegetical process establishes the exact information that the text (in this case, film) conveys or what the author (in this case, auteur) is trying to communicate.

vation, which assumes viewers' vicarious identification with the story and a double consciousness of experience it provides. We enter into the screened world "virtually" as subjective participants while also remaining in our seats as detached observers. Subjectivity and objectivity are not mutually exclusive, but they are intertwined in the film-viewing experience.

The nature of ethnographic information obtained from the film using virtual participant observation is obviously an interpreted version of the actual ethnographic data. Filmmakers are reflexive in their research process with their own personal preconceptions, which can be identified through auteur criticism. This "bias" of the filmmaker, however, is not always detrimental to the communication process; it may, in fact, help direct viewers' attention toward a particular aspect of the culture that needs immediate attention.

Another important component of the exegetical process is context criticism, which deals with the cultural context in which the film is produced, distributed, and exhibited. Film is not only a form of art; it is also an industry. Therefore, understanding the cultural dynamics within the industry is central to the process of cultural exegesis. Production values of film are normally set by studio executives, who are usually more interested in making a high return on investment than conveying credible cultural information. Independent producers, in contrast, are confined by budgets and logistics in their ability to produce and ensure authentic renditions of culture. As Devereaux and Hillerman note, "The mechanisms of mass marketing overwhelm cinemas with local meanings and smaller production budgets threaten to expunge them" (Devereaux and Hillerman 1995: 6).

Once we analyze all three components, cultural exegesis can be performed by triangulating virtual participant observation (VPO) with auteur criticism and context criticism (see fig. 3.2).

Virtual Participant Observation

In traditional ethnographic research, we interact with the subjects in their natural environment over a period of time to collect and analyze field data through the eyes of an objective observer. It is an etic perspective, an outsider's point of view, based on the criteria established by a specific theoretical framework. However, it is also important for us to participate in the culture as insiders to obtain an emic perspective, the insider's point of view, based on the criteria estab-

become a participant of their cultural experience. The focus is not on describing the behavior but on exegeting the meaning of the events and intent of the behavior.

A universal method for field research is participant observation, where the researcher becomes part of the life of the subjects and reflects on what he or she observes from "the native's point of view." (Malinowski 1961: 25) This process is envisioned as a continuum, based on the degree of our participation in the cultural experience of the subjects. On one end of the spectrum, it can be active participant observation, wherein we embrace the observed culture and experience it firsthand with the subjects. At the other extreme, nonparticipant observation, we assume the role of a completely detached observer having no direct contact with the field of study.

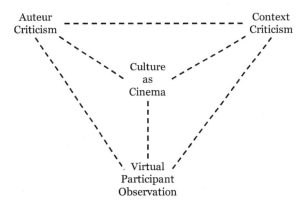

Fig. 3.2. *Cultural Exegesis of Film*

We would propose a new stance in this continuum where we enter the diegetic world of a film "virtually" to participate in the culture it depicts. The visual narrative of the film creates an "emotional event," which allows us to experience the life of the characters voyeuristically, vicariously, and viscerally (Boorstin 1995).[5] At first, it draws us into

5. Jon Boorstin explored this emotional connection between the viewers and the film, suggesting three ways in which they interact with each other. He uses the three "eyes" through which the viewers see a film as a metaphor: (1) the voyeur's eye, (2) the vicarious eye, and (3) the visceral eye. The voyeur's eye operates on a very literal worldview, trying to make sense of the logical structure of the visual story. It asks, "Is this story believable?" The vicarious eye relates to the emotional truth of the movie, as the viewers invest their heart into the lives of the characters. A good film attempts to make the viewers feel part of the story by prompting them to establish a vicarious connection with its diegetic world. It ushers the viewers into the story, allowing them to empathize with at least one of its characters. The visceral eye affects the viewers at a gut level,

their world through a compelling story line, congruently providing an emic perspective of the field. However, repeated viewing of the film creates an emotional disconnect, which helps us distance ourselves from the insiders' life and observe cultural information from an etic perspective. As we watch the film multiple times, "seeing" changes into "looking," and "experiencing" gives way to "exploration." At this point, we learn to look into the film with an "objective" eye, uncovering multiple layers of cultural symbols and their meanings embedded within the film narrative.[6]

At its core, virtual participant observation (VPO) is film analysis through an anthropological lens. We look at how the narrative, performative, and sensory elements of the film create a virtual experience and negotiate its meaning for the viewers (see methodology for film analysis in appendix 3). Ethnographic data observed from a film using VPO could be subsequently interpreted using traditional methodologies of ethnographic research. The following are some guiding questions to consider when engaging in virtual participant observation:

1. Observe kinship patterns: How does the group interaction operate among family members and relatives?
2. Observe economic systems: How do the people earn a living and carry out economic transactions?
3. Observe social structures: How do people group themselves within society and form their identity?
4. Observe political organizations: How do people control social behavior within the group, and how do they interact with members of other groups?

viewers see a film as a metaphor: (1) the voyeur's eye, (2) the vicarious eye, and (3) the visceral eye. The voyeur's eye operates on a very literal worldview, trying to make sense of the logical structure of the visual story. It asks, "Is this story believable?" The vicarious eye relates to the emotional truth of the movie, as the viewers invest their heart into the lives of the characters. A good film attempts to make the viewers feel part of the story by prompting them to establish a vicarious connection with its diegetic world. It ushers the viewers into the story, allowing them to empathize with at least one of its characters. The visceral eye affects the viewers at a gut level, placing them inside the story and letting them experience the thrill and the excitement of the moment. A movie with a visceral core involves a strong connection where viewers react even to the action of camera movements or editing techniques. It is these voyeuristic, vicarious, and visceral powers that help a film engage the viewers' minds (Boorstin 1995), making possible the process of virtual participant observation.

6. This is similar to ethnographers experiencing culture. Early on, everything is new and exciting, and they write everything down in great descriptive detail. Later, as they have observed something repeatedly, they move beyond the description to a deeper questioning of the meaning behind the behavior patterns being described. They try to appreciate the intent, the rationale behind the behavior, and how people respond or interact with it. All this moves beyond the surface/cognitive experience to the emotional and evaluative aspects of the experience, which get at what is really important for the people.

5. Observe religious systems: How do people interact with supernatural forces and transempirical structures such as faith and spirituality?
6. Observe various cultural/religious symbols used in different settings of people's daily lives: What forms of symbols are present, and what are their meanings?
7. Observe rituals and ceremonies: Who participates in these rituals and why? What are the religious themes associated with the rituals?
8. Observe mythical themes: Does the narrative refer to any myths? What plots, morals, motifs, and themes emerge from these myths, and how do they influence society?

Once cultural exegesis of film is complete, the next step is to read religion from ethnographic data. For example, from a symbolic perspective, we can look at the symbols, myths, rituals, and sacred texts to gain a comprehensive understanding of the religious perceptions in the culture. Or from a structural-functional perspective, we can classify and categorize specific aspects of culture by mapping out different elements of cultural subsystems. One of the most predominant subsystems of culture is religion, where we examine how people define the metaphysical forces that lie outside their realm of comprehension and the methods they devise to interact with these forces in meaningful ways.[7]

Auteur Criticism

Film is a collaborative medium that involves a number of contributors, making the true author of the film invisible. Auteur criticism is a methodology that responds to the challenge of identifying the artist behind the art.

In auteur criticism, it is often assumed that the personal and social history of the auteur influences the content of a film. The theory behind auteur criticism is founded on the following three assumptions (Gerstner 2003):

---

7. These subsystems include: (1) kinship systems, which indicate the ways in which people interact within a family network; (2) economic systems, which examine how the members of a society interact with their environment to earn a living; (3) social structures, which explore the way in which people group themselves and form social order; (4) political organizations, which investigate the ways in which groups control the behavior of members within them or their interaction with people outside the group; and (5) religious systems, which classify the belief and value systems associated with their collective search for meaning.

1. Even though filmmaking is a collaborative project, a film becomes a meaningful work of art when one person (auteur) exercises creative control of the project.
2. We can observe thematic and stylistic patterns emerging from an auteur's collective body of work.
3. A film is its auteur's self-expression, which means that his or her individual worldview and value systems are reflected in the film.

The key objective here is not only to identify continuity of a specific style, but also to analyze the evolution and progression of these variables in the auteur's filmography.

In the initial stages of film industry's development, studios exercised full control of the intellectual property and the subject matter. Therefore, the auteur's self-expression was often limited to the stylistic features of the film. However, as the control shifted from studios to independent producers, auteurs gained the ability to express themselves by influencing the content of the film. The director is normally considered to be the auteur of the film, according to the conventions of the film industry. However, in certain cases, screenwriters, producers, and even actors may assume auteuristic roles.

Auteur criticism begins by identifying the person who holds the most authoritative position in the filmmaking process. A number of questions need to be answered in the process: Who is the primary creative force? Who exercised authoritative control of the production process? Who takes the ultimate responsibility for the views expressed in the film? To analyze the artistic signature of the auteur, one needs an overall understanding of the auteur's body of work.

Once we study the filmmaking style of the auteur, we focus on the individual film to observe how it relates to the already-established thematic and stylistic preferences of the auteur. The following step-by-step process (Bywater and Sobchack 1989) can be helpful for auteur criticism, specifically from an anthropological perspective:

1. Identify the true auteur of the film.
2. Search for magazines, journals, DVD special features, online special features, etc. about the auteur—for example, biography, filmography, interviews, correspondence, blogs, and reviews of films produced by the auteur.
3. Locate other films produced by the auteur, and watch as many of the person's films as possible.

4. Examine these films for recurring thematic patterns, narrative features, camera style, music choice, and so on.

   a. Do they belong to the same genre? Does the auteur have a preference?
   b. Does the auteur work with the same creative partners (producers, writers, actors, cinematographers, music directors, editors, etc.)? Why or why not?
   c. What are some of the visual elements common to the films (for example, color palette, lighting, camera movement, camera angle. and editing)?
   d. What are the characteristic features of the music?
   e. How is the auteur's personal story reflected in the film's story?
   f. Do the films reflect social issues and concerns? What are the auteur's personal responses to contemporary social events?
   g. What point of view does the auteur adopt while representing the issues and concerns? What does the auteur's view tell us about his or her personal preoccupations?

5. It may be difficult to get access to filmmakers, but whenever possible, conduct interviews or ask if they would be willing to answer a list of questions via email or phone. When direct access is not feasible, read memoirs, autobiographies, letters, and other correspondence available in the public domain.

Auteur criticism functions as a reliable tool for measuring film-maker's reflexivity—one of the key factors influencing the credibility of the film's representation of a culture. The method indicates the level of subjectivity with which the auteur portrays ethnographic informa-tion in a film and clarifies whether representation of culture in the film is a part of an auteur's "agenda," is a product of authentic research, or (as in most cases) falls somewhere in between.

Context Criticism

While auteur criticism pays attention to the intended meaning of the film, context criticism focuses on its received meaning. We looked at patterns of stylistic sensibilities and cultural presuppositions of the auteur, but these variables are also influenced by the context in which the film is conceived, produced, and distributed. Cultural representation in film is invariably influenced by the "network of relationships that stretch from local sites of exhibition to global political and economic maneuvering" (Gray 2010: 138).

Context criticism looks at film as a product of social activity controlled by different networks of organizations such as production, distribution, and exhibition, which we collectively call "the film industry." We need to be aware of the relationship this industry has with other social organizations, political structures, and religious institutions. We consider the ways in which the nature of this relationship influences and, at times, controls the content of a film. If the local film industry, for example, is modeled after the studio system, where profit motive is more dominant than artistic considerations, films produced in this context are likely meant for mass entertainment. Of course, profit motive and artistic integrity can coexist in a filmmaking endeavor, but more often than not, the former trumps the latter, and the film ends up being more of a consumer product than an expression of art.

The nature of a film's social reception can be analyzed quantitatively (using scores posted on websites such as IMDb, Rotten Tomatoes, and Metacritic) or qualitatively (using questionnaires, surveys, and focus groups). A content analysis of viewers' comments in various platforms such as film reviews, fan activities, and film institution documents also may prove helpful. Statistical data on the local film industry may come from a variety of sources, such as professional associations of writers (Writers Guild of America), directors (Directors Guild of America), or producers (Producers Guild of America); government organizations that deal with media and communication; business statistics; and newspaper articles. It might be helpful to ask the following questions (Bywater and Sobchack 1989) for doing context criticism:

1. Who dominates the production? Is it studio or independent production? Is there a strategic relationship between the two?
2. What are the normal funding agencies available to the local film industry? Private or public? What are their criteria for funding a film?
3. What are the distribution models? Are there chain theaters? Is there international distribution?
4. Do people watch films in theaters or at home on computers or smartphones?

5. Is the movie an original or a spin-off? Does it use a proven formula?
6. Who owns the film? Who has a controlling interest?
7. Is this an adaptation of a literary work, which was already popular in its cultural context? What other contemporary cultural documents help us understand the film better?
8. What historical, literary, and cultural influences and values shaped the work?
9. Is there documented evidence of the social response to the film: initial screening, subsequent screening, history, policy changes in the government, public statement by an organization etc.?
10. Was the film nominated for any awards? Did the movie win any awards? What are the affiliated bodies of these awards?
11. How does the work reflect, interpret, defend, or question its sociocultural norms? Does the film conform to any existing social power structure, or does it rebel against them?
12. What is the rating of the movie? What does it reflect within the rating system of the industry?
13. How did the movie perform at the box office? How did it perform in its original context culture, and how was its performance different in other contexts?
14. Did the audience vicariously identify with the characters? What was audience members' emotional response to the film?
15. What kind of audience did the film target?
16. Did the film resonate with its viewers' personal, social, and cultural experiences?
17. What is the main purpose of the film—to teach or to entertain? Does it contribute to the artistic and cultural heritage of the society?

The investigation of a film's interaction with its spectators is important to context criticism. Audience response criticism takes into account the viewers' contribution to the task of creating meaning, apart from the meaning intended by the auteur. The effect of film on its audience cannot be predicted accurately, because it varies depending upon audience members' immediate concerns and emotional attachments.

The audience response varies considerably with the psychological state of individual viewers, so it needs to be critiqued using psychoanalytical theories. The depiction of religious values portrayed in the film reflects the dynamics between social problems and the audience members' response to their problems. The conversation is thus two-way: "Film does not contain and determine its own meaning; meaning is negotiated between the spectator and the film" (Miles 1996: 11).

Summary

Film is a culturally marked form of communication, and filmmaking is a cultural activity. Therefore, both filmmaking and film viewing can be considered a "socially structured group behavior" (Deacy 2008: 93). Deacy complains that, "while it is important to give due consideration to the themes that arise in a given film . . . insufficient attention has been accorded hitherto to the vital sense in which the film audience contributes to a 'religious' reading of the film" (2005: 5).

Postmodern theoretical frameworks in anthropology offer limitless opportunities to fashion ethnography using artistic imagination. In film, the thick description of culture takes the form of a fictional narrative enhanced by performative and sensory components. Film possesses the power to emotionally control our voyeuristic, vicarious, and visceral sensibilities, virtually transporting us into another world. This participatory experience created by the film helps us partake in the life of its characters and conduct virtual field research in its diegetic world.

Cultural exegesis looks at film from an anthropological perspective, considering it as a valid form of field research, through which ethnographic data can be collected for subsequent interpretation and representation. The heart of our methodology for cultural exegesis is virtual participant observation (VPO), where we voluntarily accept the auteur's invitation to enter into the filmic world through a process of guided imagination. As the viewing process is repeated, the point of view changes from emic to etic, reinstating the objectivity in the observation process. Virtual participant observation is complemented by auteur criticism, which gives insight into the subjectivity and reflectivity of the storyteller, and context criticism, which examines the cultural context in which the story is produced and distributed. A triangulation of VPO, auteur criticism, and context criticism indicates to what extent the cultural depiction of the film varies from that of the actual field and helps us sift out the superfluous elements that are not representative of the actual context.

4

———

The World of World Cinema

Extended Boundaries of Religious Criticism

Now more than ever we need to talk to each other, to listen to each other
and understand how we see the world, and cinema is the best medium for
doing this.
—Martin Scorsese

One of the best ways to understand a culture is to study the stories told
by its people. Cinema is arguably the most popular medium of storytelling in today's world. Cinemas of the world introduce the life of the
other in an entertaining yet engaging way, thus fostering a sense of
unity amid diversity in our global village. Films act as cultural bridges
between groups, facilitating cross-cultural communication and promoting intercultural understanding.

Film is more than images projected on a screen; film has the power
to penetrate deep into the cultural subconscious and influence the
mind of each social actor. According to Janice Rushing, "films are to the
cultural unconscious what dreams are to the personal unconscious"
(Ostwalt 2008: 43). Therefore, film both reflects and transforms the
sociocultural milieu of the context in which it is produced and consumed. This is particularly true in the case of art-house cinema, which
leaves more room for authentic self-expression of an auteur with minimum interference from the studios and marketing networks. Popular

films, in contrast, are involved in a culture-making process by inducing trend-setting norms and values in our cultural psyche. They borrow from the culture, reimagine the culture, and re-present it in the form of a new social reality. The viewers embrace this imagined cultural paradigm as their new reality and try to imitate what is seen in the filmic world, from hairstyle to lifestyle. Thus, film both reflects the culture in which it is produced and influences the one in which it is consumed.

World cinema is loaded with heavily coded cultural information that can be used as a great source for social inquiry and ethnographic investigation. This chapter takes the methodology for religious criticism developed in the previous chapters and extends it to the cinemas of the world in order to help us understand the perception of "the religious" in different cultural contexts.

Defining World Cinema

World cinema can be described as a compilation of cultural performances that draws its meaning and power from the social dramas of diverse contexts. According to cultural anthropology, religion is one of the primary driving forces of these performances; hence the study of world cinema is vital in developing an understanding of the functional dimension of religion in various cultures. Most definitions of world cinema follow subcultural categorizations of film based on their geographical placement. The following list provides the general classification of world cinema most often employed in academic circles:

1. **Hollywood cinema:** This category consists of classical American cinema produced by Hollywood studios and independent producers. Within Hollywood cinema, there are also subcategories based on culture, such as Hispanic cinema, African-American cinema, etc.
2. **European cinema:** These films are mostly produced according to Hollywood conventions, but thematically, European films center specifically on the auteur's artistic expression.
3. **National cinema:** This category encompasses indigenous films produced by different countries of the world, depending on the source of funding, language of production, etc. The classification is unique to films produced by citizens of non-Western countries, which are often categorized according to language of production.
4. **Diasporic cinema:** These are films produced by auteurs in a

diasporic culture with a strong link to their native culture or about some aspect of the diasporic experience.

5. **Transnational cinema:** This category includes multi-sited films that target global audience and are normally coproduced by different countries.

6. **Third cinema:** The counter-cinema movement (primarily in Latin American countries) attempts to rebel against the dominant ideologies and practices in popular films produced by revolutionary, experimental artists.

World cinema is often used as a collective term to describe the sum total of all films produced outside the Hollywood industry. However, this categorization assumes that all non-Western films share similar characteristics, which is not the case. Therefore, we would adopt Lúcia Nagib's definition of world cinema which puts cinemas of all cultures on equal footing:

> World cinema is simply the cinema of the world. It has no center. It is not the other, but it is us. It has no beginning and no end, but is a global process. World cinema, as the world itself, is circulation. World cinema is not a discipline, but a method, a way of cutting across film history according to waves of relevant films and movements, thus creating flexible geographies. (2006: 35)

In this book, world cinema is a collective forum of all cinemas. Each member of world cinema represents a unique ethnographic context in which it can be equally conceived, produced, viewed, and conditioned for scientific investigation.

Today many thriving film industries around the world exist outside of Hollywood. According to the statistical portait in figure 4.1, India has the largest film industry in the world—nearly double that of Hollywood. Nigerian film industry, often known as Nollywood, also is bigger than Hollywood, but it is not considered for comparison, due to statistical limitations.[1] Although Latin American and Iranian films are not included in the figure, many films produced in these regions are winning prestigious awards and accolades in the international scene. As figure 4.1 illustrates, Hollywood is no longer the only reference point for studying world cinema.

---

1. Nigerian films are difficult to account for because most of them are direct-to-DVD productions. The following documentaries provide some inside information of the industry: *This Is Nollywood* by Franco Sacchi and Robert Caputo (2006), and *Welcome to Nollywood* by Jamie Meltzer (2007).

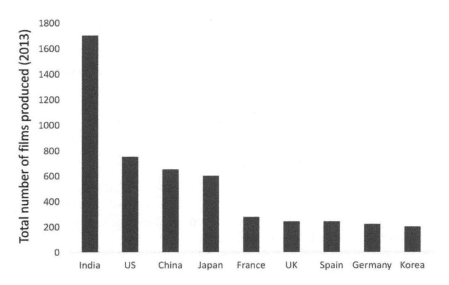

Fig. 4.1. *The Leading Film Industries of the World*

Traditionally, academic writing on world cinema has focused on European cinema with a passing look at Latin America or Japan. These industries are unique in that they have direct access to Hollywood distribution networks and unprecedented exposure in the Hollywood industry. Some of the A-list filmmakers in Hollywood, for instance, are originally from Latin America. Alejandro González Iñárritu won two consecutive Oscars for best director of *The Revenant* (2015) and *Birdman* (2014). Emmanuel Lubezki won three consecutive Oscar awards for best cinematography in *The Revenant* (2015), *Birdman* (2014), and *Gravity* (2013). Both Iñárritu and Lubezki are Mexican born.

On the other side of the globe, Japan has one of the oldest film industries in the world and has produced auteurs familiar to the West. Akira Kurosawa's repertoire includes *Ran* (1985), *Kagemusha* (1980), and *Ikiru* (1952). Yasujirô Ozu has also had a long history in cinema, including *Tokyo Story* (1953), *Good Morning* (1959), and *Bakushû* (1951). Hayao Miyazaki's *Spirited Away* (2001) and *Princess Mononoke* (1997) are notable contributions to world cinema as well. Today, Japan is mostly known in the Western world for its stylistic influence in specific industrial segments like animation (Japanese anime) and horror film franchises.

In China, a booming film industry has enjoyed unprecedented growth in recent years. The film industry was originally state owned, with the government controlling the financing, production, distribution, and exhibition networks. These films were typically branded "main melody" (*zhu xuanlu*), which were films that promoted the patriotic principles espoused by the state. The studio system, however, was slowly disintegrating, giving rise to the emergence of more independent producers. Films like Chen Kaige's *Yellow Earth* (1984), Zhang Yimou's *Red Sorghum* (1987) and *Raise the Red Lantern* (1991), and Ping He's *Red Firecracker Green Firecracker (1993)* have received critical acclaim around the world, while popular films such as Chen Kaige's *Farewell My Concubine* (1993), Ang Lee's *Crouching Tiger, Hidden Dragon* (2000), and Zhang Yimou's *Hero* (2002) and *House of Flying Daggers* (2004) have enjoyed wider international releases and box office success.

Farther east, the Korean film industry is demonstrating steady advancement and becoming increasingly competitive in the international market. Korea has been influenced by Japanese colonization, national division, civil war, and authoritative military governments, which have become recurring themes in Korean films. In 1997, *The Contact* by Chang Youn-hyun saw a blockbuster performance in the domestic market, leading up to the groundbreaking success of Kang Je-gyu's *Shiri* (1999). Kim Ki-duk, known for his visually striking cinematography in *The Isle* (2000), was one of the first Korean filmmakers to become well known internationally, while Lee Chang-dong won critical acclaim (the best-director award) at the Venice film festival for *Oasis* (2002). Chan-wook Park's *JSA (Joint Security Area)* (2000) was also a huge success, surpassing all earlier box office records. A number of other successful Korean films, such as *My Sassy Girl* (2001) and *Oldboy* (2003), have even experienced Hollywood remakes.

Even a peripheral look at major film industries across the world can become too exhaustive and cumbersome for academic writing. Therefore, rather than going for a descriptive overview of world cinema, this book focuses on the largest film industry in the world, India's Bollywood, as a case study of cultural dynamics within world cinema.

Bollywood: India's Film Industry

With over a thousand films produced annually, India houses the largest film industry in the world. Bollywood is a nickname given to Indian films, but in reality, it only represents the Hindi film industry based in Mumbai. Few know that Indian cinema encompasses other streams as well, including art-house cinema and regional cinema. Yet Bollywood remains the most popular expression of Indian cinema, and it enthrones itself as a trendsetter in India's popular culture. Bollywood films now claim international releases, are regularly screened in major film festivals, and often win international awards.

The history of Indian film begins in 1913 with Dhundiraj Govind Phalke's *Raja Harishchandra* (1913). The film is a pious depiction of the story of Lord Krishna. Most productions of the earlier times were formula films embellished with frivolous songs and dance sequences. The films were meant to "entertain" the general public, who needed an escape from the harsh realities of daily life.

In the 1950s, a new-wave movement entered India, mostly through the regional cinema of Bengal. Satyajit Ray's first film, *Pather Panchali* (1955), won the award for "the best human document" at Cannes Film Festival. Ritwik Ghatak made films such as *Ajantrik* (1958), *Meghe Dhaka Tara* (1960), and *Suvarna Rekha* (1965) with themes centered on India's freedom struggle, partition of the state of Bengal, and its socio-psychological repercussions in the country. Shyam Benegal followed suit with a series of films such as *Ankur* (1974) and *Nishant* (1975). Both films featured vivid depictions of village life and rural values. Mrinal Sen alluded to Marxism as a solution to the country's social issues in his films such as *Bhuvan Shome* (1970), *Interview* (1970), and *Mrigayaa* (1976).

Similar movements took place in other regional cinemas based in south India. The Malayalam film industry based in Kerala, and the Kannada film industry, based in Karnataka, also produced films that show realistic depictions of ordinary people's relationship with social, political, and religious institutions. In addition, foreign films about India have been produced that could be included as part of the history of Indian cinema. The rich cultural heritage of the country and its beautiful locations attracted several filmmakers from various parts of the world. Indo-American joint productions by Ismail Merchant and James Ivory, *The Householder* (1963) and *Shakespeare Wallah* (1965), received critical acclaim and box office success, while *Gandhi* (1982), an Indo-British coproduction, won eight Oscars including best picture and best director, a success that was recently repeated by *Slumdog Millionaire* (2008), another Indo-British coproduction, by winning another eight Academy Awards, including best picture and best director.

Bollywood films are known for a style called *masala*,[2] blending multiple genres into a single film and creating a fusion of comedy, musical, drama, and action films into one narrative. These films typically run

2. Originally a name for Indian spice mix.

between two and three hours. "We Indians like our pleasure in small doses," says Vasudev. "Forty-five minutes of love and fun must be followed by suffering. It is now time for sacrifice. . . . Our hero must sacrifice his dream career, and almost ends up losing his girl. In the end, of course, everything works out, and they live happily ever after" (Panjwani 2006: 26). The plots of Bollywood films are simple and predictable, often consisting of "patently preposterous narratives, overblown dialogues, exaggeratedly stylized acting . . . [and a] disregard for psychological characterization, history, geography, and even sometimes camera placement rules."[3]

Music plays a major role in revenue generation for Bollywood films. The box office success of a film usually depends on the popularity of the sound track. The songs are generally prerecorded by professional playback singers, with actors later lip-synching the lyrics. A typical Bollywood film tends to have five to seven choreographed dance routines, which are accompanied by a troupe of supporting dancers and instantaneously shifting locations and costumes. The sexualized bodies of the heroine and the voyeuristic gaze of the camera are interesting traits in dance sequences. Some dance scenes can be erotic with sexual innuendos conveyed through subtle glances and gestures.

Music also performs a narrative function in Bollywood by participating in the storytelling process. "Songs elaborate on the discourse in the tale," says Gayatri Chatterji. "Its discursive property invigorates the theme and narrative and it enhances the meaning, feeling and 'rasa' of the performance" (2008: 105). In the same vein, Jyotika Virdi also notes that the song sequence performs various functions within the narrative: "A song can be marshaled to advance the story at a rhapsodic juncture within the narrative or to convey moods—love, passion, separation, longing—or the lyrics may simply be a part of the extra-diegetic music overlaid upon a montage sequence, summarizing the narrative" (2003: 189).

It is also common to see the characters breaking out into a song-and-dance number in the middle of a conversation. Such transitions from dialogue to song, according to the conventions of Western film criticism, break the narrative and disrupt the storytelling process. But in Bollywood films, this structure is "an important component of the episodic narratives, which is in synch with the fact that music and rasa may be enjoyed serially" (Chatterji 2008: 91).

---

3. Thomas 1985, as cited in Hill and Gibson 2000: 157.

The studio system has now disintegrated in Bollywood, with private investors acting as primary financiers for most films. It is also an open secret that the funding for many projects comes from the Mumbai underworld.[4] Today, Indian films are often financed by major Hollywood studios, thanks to the unique niche Bollywood has created in the world of music, dance, and fashion.

Religion in Indian Cinema

Cinema, like religion, streams through the lifeblood of Indian culture. One could find just as many movie theaters in a typical Indian village as there are temples, mosques, or churches. The posters of movie stars adorn the shrines of Indian homes along with the idols of Hindu gods and goddesses. From the street art of the slums to the iconography of the temples, its pervasive influence on human imagination makes cinema a religious experience for the people of India. Chatterji refers to "cultural traditions that arise from religious thoughts and practices and shape cinema in India" (2008: 92).

The secular and the sacred are intermingled to the extent that a separation between them is virtually impossible. According to Dwyer, "A striking feature of modern India is the presence of the religious, whether in images, gesture, language, festivals, rituals and so on" (2006: 140). One cannot interpret the nature of a cultural phenomenon without first understanding the religious context within which it takes place. Indian films, therefore, retain "the discursive nature of religious narratives and conduct social criticism while staying within the bounds of religious faith" (Chatterji 2008: 88).

Western critics often look at Bollywood as an exotic spectacle or as mindless entertainment. But in India, film is a social institution that reflects and transforms cultural realities. As Kothari puts it, "Indian cinema, despite all its peculiarities, has been a reflection of the socio-economic, political, and cultural changes that took place in the country" (2013: 17). According to Dwyer, Bollywood reflects "the kaleidoscopic heterogeneity of Indian culture" (2006: 27), and its interpretations of India are a reliable guide to understanding the nation's changing hopes and dreams. Madhava Prasad (1998) describes Bollywood films as articulations of identity and Indianness, which promote the

---

4. In 2001, the Central Bureau of Investigation seized all prints of the movie *Chori Chori Chupke Chupke* after the movie was found to be funded by members of the Mumbai underworld. Vijay Singh, "Bharat Shah Sentenced, but Won't Have to Spend Time in Prison," *Rediff*, October 1, 2003, rediff.com.

ideology of the nation-state of India and engage in the process of creating national identity. Virdi believes that Bollywood films provide a fascinating account of social history and cultural politics as "they configure the concept of 'nation' in post-independent India by creating an imagined universe, with the idea of 'nation' as its focal point" (2003: 108). Indian film is an "emotional register" that functions as a virtual teleprompter for reading the script called nation (Virdi 2003).

A common theme that appears in Bollywood films is the archetype of the Mother, often used as a metaphor for the country itself. The term Mother India (*Bharat Mata*) first appeared in films as an instrument to unify the diverse cultures of Indianness.[5] The caring and nurturing mother eventually became a symbol of India in defiance of the British rule. The patriotic portrayal of India as a mother-goddess implied that it is also a religious duty to participate in the struggle to defend the nation.

The idea of family, another recurring theme in Bollywood films, also alludes to the sociocultural realities in India. As Virdi notices, Indian films tend to "deploy family as a symbol of the nation" (Virdi 2003) to discuss the social history and cultural politics of the country. Family in India is a larger unit than the nuclear family of the West; it consists of grandparents, grandchildren, uncles, aunts, cousins, nephews, and nieces. It can also transcend blood relationships to include brotherhood and fraternity. It is common to see biological siblings turning into bitter enemies while a friend, or a total stranger, assumes the sibling's role in the "family." The concept of *bhai* (brother) or *bahen* (sister) is an earned status, which even challenges the boundaries of the notorious caste system in the country.

The role of religion in Bollywood is not confined to the diegetic world of the film; even the practical aspects of the production process are invariably influenced by the religious nature of Indian culture. Tejaswini Ganti, in her detailed ethnographic report on the Bollywood film industry recounts "the presence of Hindu rituals, which have become incorporated into production routines" (2012: 156). She observes how astrologers are consulted before finalizing the production and how priests are invited to perform elaborate ceremonies before the commencement of film shooting. It is also common for Bol-

5. In 1936, a Bharat Mata temple was built in Benaras and was inaugurated by Gandhi. He hoped that the worship of Bharat Mata would serve as a platform for people of all religions, castes, and creeds to promote religious unity and peace. It still remains as a symbol of the vision of a unified motherland in Indian nationalist agenda. *Bharat mata ki jay* (Hail to Mother India) is a common slogan heard in political and religious platforms.

lywood films to start with opening shots paying homage to favorite deities, accompanied by sacred mantras in the sound track.

Bollywood films tend to be stereotypical in their representation of religious communities. The lead characters in most films are upper-caste, north Indian Hindu males, with others playing mostly supporting roles. Lower castes and outcasts (Dalits) appear in lead roles usually when it is a "message" film.[6] Sikhs and Jains are at times portrayed as subsects of Hinduism, while Christians are mostly comedians or villains. The church buildings, however, are portrayed as a safe haven for people of all religions. The common thread of the religious message is that all religions can peacefully coexist. This is metaphorically depicted in the classic film *Amar, Akbar and Anthony* (1977), where three brothers separated at birth are brought up as Hindu, Muslim, and Christian, and in the end are reunited as a family.

Dwyer classifies Indian cinema in three genres based on their depiction of religion. Mythological films narrate stories of gods and goddesses from popular Hindu myths and religious epics; examples are *Raja Harichandra* (1913), *Sree Krishna Janma* (1918), *Kaliya Mardan* (1919), *Ram Rajya* (1943), and *Jai Snathoshi Ma* (1975). Devotional films tell stories of historical persons whose lives are defined by spiritual experiences they have had through divine encounters, as seen in *Sant Tukaram* (1936) and *Sant Dnyaneshwar* (1940). Islamicate films are "Muslim socials," which tell the stories within the social and cultural setting of the Islamic faith; examples are *Salim Lagde Pe Mat Ro* (1989) and *Nazeem* (1995). Dwyer suggests, "A removal of these [religious] elements will [make the Hindi film] seem not only unrealistic, but would also take away from its emotions, its spectacle and so on" (2006: 140).

Mythological criticism reveals the organic relationship between film and mythology in Bollywood. Amitab Bachchan, one of the demigods of Bollywood, once said, "Leading men in Hindi cinema are modern manifestations of the great heroes from our two great epics, the Mahabharat and Ramayana. They are always invisible and they always win in the end" (Wright 2007:150). Virdi describes popular screen characterization of women in Bollywood as "mythology's timeless cultural resources" (2003: 60). Most films tend to have an allegorical structure, which connects the main characters to different archetypes of Hindu mythology. Direct confrontation between good and evil is a common theme in Bollywood films, where characters represent ethical arche-

---

6. *Lagaan* (2001) is a classic example.

types. The hero is the personification of all virtues, whereas the villain is the incarnation of all vices. Ritwik Ghatak (1925–1976), one of the greatest filmmakers of India, said that "if you want to preach a social message, you can't do it without mythology" (Vasudev 1986: 25).[7] Armes, when critiquing Ghatak's movies, observes that "at the level of plot events, these films are contemporary tales, but underlying this contemporaneity is a complex allegorical structure relating to the archetypes of Indian mythology in ways that constitute a critique of conventional Indian filmic approaches to myth" (1997: 308). The heroes and heroines of the film metamorphose into gods and goddesses in the subconscious of the viewers and the message conveyed by the film, thus becoming a prophetic utterance. In this way, film not only recreates mythologies, but also constructs new mythologies for the next generation.

The sacramental value of film is perceived through the act of *darshan,* a phenomenological category in religion that describes both seeing and being seen by the divine. *Darshan* is originally used in Hindu worship as "experiencing the presence of the divine through the act of seeing an image of a god or saint" (Wright 2007: 151). When devotees perform *darshan,* they come into direct contact with the deities. The gods are believed to see the worshippers as well. Therefore, *darshan* is also something given by the deities to the devotees, and it consists of "contact between devotee and deity . . . exchanged through the eyes" (Eck 1998: 7).

Darshan is not a simple act of looking at the depiction of the gods. According to Plate, *darshan* takes place within "a series of ritual rules that *frame* the experience for the viewer, providing boundaries for *what* is seen and *how* objects are seen" (2002: 162). *Darshan* is both giving and receiving a "view," which Wright describes as a "two way look" or a "dynamic mutual exchange" (2007, 151).[8] The audience looks at images as if they are literal manifestations of the divine, and their gaze becomes an act of worship. According to the psychoanalytical film theories developed by Jacques Lacan, the viewers of a film become subjects of a "gaze" when the images on the screen become the object of their desire. At this point, the images cater to the longing of the subjects,

---

7. Vasudev notes, "Repeated allusions to Indian mythology give [Ghatak's] films a density for Indian audiences, an impenetrable quality for those unaware of them" (1986, 25).
8. For example, when Christians approach a film like Mel Gibson's *Passion of the Christ* (2004), their focus is on "seeing," not "watching." They already know the story, and hence the religious content of the film is not of primary concern. They are there to participate in a religious spectacle that provides a sensual experience of their faith.

making them receive a view of the filmic world. This process is illusory, of course, but it still has a powerful emotional impact on the viewers. As cinema is influenced by religion, therefore, the meaning of religion is also mediated through cinema.

Summary

World cinema artfully depicts the stories emerging from the cultural psyche of the world. Culture is thickly described in cinema, using a combination of fictional narrative, performative elements, and audio-visual components. Even if the scientific authenticity of cultural representation through a film is disputed, world cinema can function as a valuable source of ethnographic data, which can be subsequently decoded and analyzed using scientific methodologies.

There are, of course, differing opinions in academia on the ethnographic authenticity of cinema, but even its harshest critics would agree that film can be used in ethnographic research as a "datum of culture" (Ruby 1975). There was a time social scientists considered film merely as "illustrations" of written texts, but they have now realized that film can be a unique communicative vehicle for ethnographic knowledge and a powerful pedagogical source in religious studies. It can engage the audience more effectively than text at emotional, subliminal, and even ideological levels, so that a teacher offering movies "as material for cultural and theological analysis . . . is thus handling influential, cultural products that are varyingly received critically but are nevertheless examples of good-quality popular culture" (Marsh 2008: 156).

As a result, different standards and sets of assumptions should be used in criticizing movies from different parts of the world. A "culture studies approach to film . . . [should] concentrate on interrogating, and being led by, the specific cultural formations (including religious ones) implicated in a particular film" (Wright 2007: 144). Theological criteria for critiquing a film should be derived from its own cultural context, and therefore religious criticism of film should have an "extensive integration with culture studies" (Wright 2007: 25). In the next chapter, we test the validity and reliability of the methodology by applying the procedure to a film from the world of diasporic Bollywood.

A significant number of films in Bollywood tell explicit religious stories, and the viewers in India are attuned to recognize the religious symbolism hidden under the juxtaposition of image, sound, and music in Indian films. This, in turn, helps them decipher the socio-political arguments underneath the plot events. Religion, notes Dwyer, "has been ever present as the dominant worldview of Indian cinema, not just represented directly by divine presences or by religious communities, but also manifested in ways of creating an ideal world through the individual, the family and the society" (Dwyer 2006: 2).

5

The Elements Trilogy

A Cultural Critique of India

I seriously wanted to break the stereotypes of India, the "exotic" India of
the Raj and the princes and the mysticism. . . . The exotic India doesn't
really exist.
—Deepa Mehta

To test the validity of the methodology we proposed in chapter 4, we
now turn to a concrete example, the Elements Trilogy, an acclaimed
film series by Indo-Canadian filmmaker Deepa Mehta. The series was
selected based on its reputation in the academic circles, as well as the
critical acclaim it received in the industry. It is widely regarded as a
cultural critique of India and has been featured as a pedagogical tool
in the academic platform. It has also received substantially high rank-
ing from film viewers in popular film review sites such as IMDb, Rotten
Tomatoes, and Metacritic.

We will consider the Elements Trilogy as a "virtual field" in which we
conduct field research using virtual participant observation. Authenticity of the observed information will be evaluated in chapter 6
against data gathered from the actual field (India) through a case study
method. In chapter 7, a comparison of the ethnographic data collected
from the virtual field and the actual field will demonstrate the working
of our methodology for religious criticism.

The Elements Trilogy

The Elements Trilogy can be described as the story of India's socio-cultural evolution in reverse order. The three films of the series track the country from its present state as an emerging global economy to its primordial existence as one of the most ancient civilizations in the world.

Fire (1996), the first film of the series, places us in the context of modern India, where the cherished traditions of the past are threatened by the overpowering intrusion of pop culture, primarily imported from the West. The story takes place in New Delhi: the capital city of India, where the invisible forces of globalization are always in tension with the cultural heritage of the country. *Eqrth* (1999), the second film of the series, takes us back to 1947, a turning point in the political history of India, where the country finds itself in a cultural vacuum created by the departure of the British Empire and its division into Hindu and Muslim territories. The story is set in Lahore, a city in the blurry border between the Hindu-dominated India and the Muslim-dominated Pakistan, in the backdrop of a civil war that erupts as a result of political chaos. *Water* (2005), the final film of the series, goes further back to 1930s, when the subcontinent experiences the birthing pains of an emerging republic, through a powerful revitalization movement led by Gandhi. The story plays out in a fictional city called Rawalpur, modeled after Varanasi, the religious capital of India. The film unfolds the tragic story of a group of widows' struggle for survival in the holy city and their fight against the social stigmas and cultural taboos endorsed by religion.

Fire

Fire (see fig. 5.1, gallery) opened at the 1996 Toronto International Film Festival, where it won the People's Choice Award. In India, it was subject to fierce criticism, even demands for an immediate ban on the film. Protesters stormed into movie theaters, seized film prints, and even set theater buildings ablaze. Many religious and political leaders gleefully endorsed these violent protests against the film. "I congratulate them [the protesters] for what they have done," declared Manohar Joshi, the chief minister of Maharashtra. "The film's theme is alien to our culture" (Jain and Raval 1998: 78). *Fire* was, however, rereleased after a second review by the censor board of India and continued screenings without any major issues.

Fire opens with a prologue, introducing us to the protagonist, Radha as a little girl. In a lush green meadow peppered with bright yellow sunflowers, she is listening to the rhyming verses of a folk tale:

> A long time ago there were people living high up in the mountains. They had never seen the sea. They had heard about it. But never seen it. And this made them feel very sad. Then an old woman in the village said: "Don't be sad. What you can't see, you can see. You just have to see without looking. . . . Radha do you understand?"

The life of Radha (played as an adult by Shabana Azmi) unfolds as a metaphorical pilgrimage toward the sea, which she is trying to "see without looking." As the film begins, she is bound by (an arranged) marriage to an emotionally distant husband, Ashok (Kulbhushan Kharbanda). She has failed to fulfill her primary "duty" as a wife, which is to bear children for her husband. A disappointed Ashok withdraws to a life of celibacy and renunciation under the tutelage of Swamiji, a local Hindu monk. In a loveless, sexless marriage, Radha's role is relegated to that of a traditional housemaid, who cooks, cleans, and attends to the needs of other family members. Jathin (Javed Jaffrey), Ashok's only brother, is a rebel who loves kung fu movies and Western music. But he does not have the courage to confront his older brother. Beeji (Kushal Rekhi), their mother, may be paralyzed and bedridden, yet she is the matriarch of the family, who controls everything that happens in the family.

The well-oiled mechanism of the joint family system begins to collapse when Jathin, who is madly in love with a Chinese immigrant, Judy, is forced to marry another woman against his will. His wife, Sita (Nandita Das), may appear naive and even childish when we first meet her, but these are precisely the same virtues that make her dangerous. She is oblivious to the rules and regulations that hold the family system together in a delicate balance. She fancies herself to be a movie star, dances to the beats of Western music, dresses up in men's clothes, and even tries to steal a smoke from Jathin's cigarette pack at times. When she discovers her husband's ongoing affair with another woman, Sita does not explode like a typical melodramatic Bollywood heroine. She rather chooses to enjoy the fair share of liberty this broken relationship endows on her. Instead of retreating to her servile role as a traditional housewife, she defines her role in the family system by demanding equal rights and privileges.

It is at this point that the emotionally deprived sisters-in-law, Radha and Sita, start drawing themselves closer to each other. Their search for intimacy and emotional connection evolve into a physical relationship, which eventually leads to sharing not only their minds and souls, but their bodies as well. Mehta maintains that the film has little to do with pushing sexual boundaries. It is rather a critique of the social structures (such as the joint family system), which denigrate individuals as nothing but machines that perform their duty. In the emotional core of the film, it is about the desperate longing for self-expression shared by every individual in every culture. "The struggle between tradition and individual expression is one that takes place in every culture," Mehta insists, "*Fire* deals with this specifically in the context of Indian society."[1]

Earth

The second film of the trilogy, *Earth* (see fig. 5.2, gallery), was released in 1998. Though it dealt with an equally provocative issue, the India-Pakistan separation, *Earth* escaped without much controversy. The film was a box office success, and it also won awards including the Prix Premiere de Public at the Festival du film Asiatiquede Deauville, France, and the Critics' Award at the Schermid' Amore International Film Festival.

Earth tells the story of brotherhood and rivalry between different religious communities in India through the eyes of a little girl named Lenny (Maia Sethna). She is the only child of an upper-class aristocratic family in British India. She has a babysitter, Shanta (Nandita Das), who often walks her to a park in the neighborhood. In this park, they befriend a group of local men—a community that functions as a microcosm of the Indian society: Hindus, Muslims, and Sikhs coming together to form one big family. Lenny is a Farsi, an Indian sect that traces its ancestors to Persian immigrants in Iran. Although their official religion is Zoroastrianism, the Farsi community maintains a neutral relationship with all religious groups in India.

Shanta's charm and beauty attract many young men to her, particularly Lenny's personal hero, "the Ice Candy Man," Dil Nawaz (Aamir Khan). Shanta, however, falls for Hassan the masseur (Rahul Khanna),

---

1. From the director's note on *Fire*.

forming the proverbial love triangle. The romantic tension is intensi-
fied by the fact that Shanta is a Hindu but both Dil Nawas and Hassan
are Muslims.

When the British decide to leave India, they divide the subcontinent
into two separate countries, India and Pakistan.[2] India is called Hindus-
tan (the land of Hindus), and Pakistan is declared an Islamic republic.
The Hindus who live in Pakistan and the Muslims who live in India are
driven out of their homes, triggering a civil war between two religious
communities. Hindus and the Muslims turn against each other, while
the Sikhs are caught in the crossfire. This strife eventually affects the
relationships among the men of the group, who consider themselves
to be part of one family. Friends turn against friends, and brothers
become enemies. The once-charming Ice Candy Man suddenly becomes
a savage hunter, wandering in the streets in search of his prey. Hassan
implores the group members to stand by each other, but the voice of
reason is powerless in a war fueled by religious fanatics. During a series
of catastrophic events set in motion by the brutal riots, the romance
between Hassan and Shanta heads on to a collision course.

Earth is based on the novel *Cracking India* (1988), written by Bapsi Sidhwa, a Pakistani immigrant to the United States. As an Indian immigrant to Canada, Mehta finds in Sidhwa an ideal partner to collaborate
for the story of this sectarian war that tore apart their motherland.
The two women join together to unravel the idiosyncratic relationship
between politics and nationality, and eventually confront the viewers
with profound questions on religious self-image and cultural identity.
In the end, the film does not presume to know the answer; neither does
it lay the blame on politics or religion. Instead, it leaves the viewers
with the burden of finding their own answers and making their own
conclusions.

Water

Water (see fig. 5.3, gallery) was destined to be controversial right from
its conception. Even before the film was taken up for production,
Hindu fundamentalists aired complaints about its portrayal of Indian
widows and their relationship with the society. The Indian nationalist
party Vishwa Hindu Parishad (VHP) alleged that the film was "an
attempt to misplace the identity and character [of the widows] by pre-

---

2. The repercussions of this decision continue to this day, as India and Pakistan consider themselves
archenemies across a common border.

senting them as a laughing stock to movie watchers in the Western world." Ashok Singhal, the leader of the VHP, commented, "Even if the government allowed the filmmaker to start shooting of the film, the people would resist the move." A Hindu cleric, Shankaracharya Swami Swarupanand Saraswati, criticized the government for giving a permit to shoot the film, since it was "an insult to Indian culture and to womanhood" (Reporter 2000).

The day after the film commenced shooting in Varanasi, an angry mob stormed the location, attacked the film crew, and ransacked the set. They also organized street demonstrations, burning Mehta's effigy in the public. In the end, the military had to intervene to restore law and order. Mehta was forced a shut down the set, fearing the safety of her crew members. "In many ways I felt I was watching a movie." Mehta recollects, "I was scared. I had never seen so many machine guns. I had never had such immediate physical threats or death threats that I was the focus of, and I must say I was really upset. Upset sounds too good, I was devastated. And it took me a year or more to get out of it."[3]

When Mehta decided to reshoot *Water* after five years, she kept the project a top secret and recreated the set in Sri Lanka. She also chose a pseudonym as the working title in order to avoid any possible interference from India. The film was debuted at the Toronto International Film Festival in 2005 and became an instant favorite of both critics and audience. It picked up three Genie Awards and a series of film festival prizes all over the world. *Water* was eventually was brought to the international limelight when the Academy of Motion Picture Arts and Sciences nominated the film for the prestigious Oscars (2007) in the best-foreign-film category.

The story of *Water* is set in 1938, a mercurial time in the political and social history of India. The colonial power is on the verge of collapse, and a new republic is beginning to emerge. A prophetic figure emerges on the scene, spearheading the face of this radical movement. He is Mahatma (Great Soul) Gandhi, a leader who believes that political freedom alone will not suffice for liberation, but the country needs to be healed from its cultural wounds inflicted by the ancient customs and traditions.

The protagonist of the story is Chuyia (Sarala), an eight-year-old girl

3. Excerpts from Phillips, R. and W. Alahakoon (2000). "Hindu chauvinists block filming of Deepa Mehta's Water." Retrieved August 12, 2016. https://www.wsws.org/en/articles/2000/02/film-f12.html.

who is a victim of the notorious custom of child marriage. Her husband dies unexpectedly, leaving her to be a "widow." Chuyia is consigned to a widow ashram located on the bank of the Ganges, where she is forced to spend the rest of her life isolated from the society.

Madhumati (Manorama), the matriarch of the ashram, is ready to go to any extreme in the battle for existence. She even offers Kalyani (Lisa Ray), a beautiful young widow, as a prostitute to the rich customers across the river for their economic survival. Narayan (John Abraham), a devout follower of Gandhi, falls in love with Kalyani and decides to marry her against the prohibitions on the remarriage of widows. To keep the business going, Madhumati now has to find a new prostitute, and her evil eyes fall on Chuyia. Shakunthala (Seema Bishwas), her guardian angel in the ashram, jumps to her rescue, but the intervention comes perhaps a bit too late. In the end, Shakunthala carries the traumatized Chuyia to Gandhi, the only place of refuge known to her. There is a new realization that one needs to choose the voice of conscience over that of tradition to find true liberation.

Deepa Mehta as an Auteur

Mehta is an Indo-Canadian filmmaker. She was born in Amritsar, an Indian city bordering Pakistan. It was her father, a film distributor and a theater owner, who ushered her into the enchanting world of cinema. Mehta describes this initiation in the following words: "I must have been just about six years. I stopped to feel the screen. It was made out of fabric. I couldn't understand how could something that I could touch, and was made out of cloth make me cry. The picture and the cloth never came together until that moment. That was quiet a revelation" (personal interview, June 12, 2013).

Mehta spent most of her childhood in Amritsar until going to a boarding school in New Delhi. After receiving a master's degree in philosophy from the University of New Delhi, she chose to become a storyteller rather than going for a PhD program in social science.

Mehta's first assignment was with an independent production house called Cinematic Workshop, which made documentary films for the government of India. She started as a sound equipment operator but soon got promoted to camera work, and later got into the edit suit, slowly but surely building expertise in all aspects of the production process.

In 1973 Mehta married Paul Saltzman, a Canadian filmmaker, and immigrated to Canada. Since Saltzman himself was an acclaimed artist and filmmaker, Mehta struggled to come out of his shadow. In the 1970s, the Canadian film industry was not open to ethnic minorities in general and to women in particular. The difficulties in becoming acculturated to a new country created ripple effects in her personal life as well. The couple parted ways not long after the birth of their only daughter, Devyani Saltzman. At the time of the divorce, the eleven-year-old Devyani chose to live with her father, which probably created a deep emotional scar in Mehta's mind. However, the mother and daughter later found reconciliation and redemption—a story that is poignantly portrayed in Devyani's book, *Shooting Water* (2007), which also catalogs the production details of *Water* and the controversies surrounding the film.

The filmmaking process is a very personal endeavor for Mehta. She considers herself completely responsible for both the success and the failure of her films. "The mistakes are mine; I can't blame anyone," says Mehta. "And the credits are mine; nobody can take that away from me. It is my film." She is certainly open to suggestions from her trusted team members, but commitment to a personal vision is the hallmark of her storytelling method. "It is a question of my personal integrity," Mehta continues. "I have a story I want to tell. This is something I really felt. How to remain true to the story" (personal interview, June 12, 2013). This unflinching personal commitment to a story is one of the defining characteristics of an auteur. The key strategy for maintaining objectivity in a collaborative process is keeping a consistent team whose members understand and appreciate the creative vision of the director. Mehta considers her team a community that can read her mind and appreciate her creative vision. Since most of the team members have been working with her for decades, she can speak to them "in shorthand."

Mehta's career as an auteur began in 1991, when she produced and directed her first feature film, *Sam and Me*, which told the story of an elderly Jewish man and his friendship with a young Indian immigrant. The film debuted at the Cannes Film Festival with an honorable mention by the jury. The critical success of this film paved her way to Hollywood, where she received an invitation from none other than George Lucas himself to direct two episodes of his television series, *Young Indiana Jones Chronicles*, which aired in 1992 and 1994. Back in Canada, Mehta collaborated with Jessica Tandy and Bridget Fonda to create her second feature film, *Camilla* (1994), the story of two women who shared a common passion to pursue their vocations in music. Unfortunately, the critics snubbed the film, with one describing it as "too arbitrary and disorganized to recommend" (Ebert 1995).

In 1996 Mehta released *Fire*, the first film of the Elements Trilogy, followed by the second film, *Earth*, in 1998. We have already discussed the controversy surrounding these films and the violent protest that followed when shooting for *Water* commenced shooting in 2000. Mehta returned to Canada after this incident and spent the next four years engaged in a soul-searching process. During this period, she made *Bollywood-Hollywood* (2002), a lighthearted comedy about an Indo-Canadian business executive who hires a female escort to pose as his fiancée. The film was very uncharacteristic of Mehta's style, but it was an instant success at the box office. It bagged five Genie Awards (the Canadian equivalent of the Academy Awards), including best picture, but more importantly, provided her with the confidence and conviction she badly needed at that point in time.

Mehta's next film was the much-anticipated adaptation of an acclaimed Canadian novel, *The Republic of Love* (2003) by Carol Shields, which told the story of an unconventional relationship between a radio host and a young admirer. Mehta said, "I discovered that I had to treat Carol's deceptively simple story line as if it were a recipe for an exotic dish I had to cook! Fragrant, spicy, light to the palate and yet substantial and filling."[4] Despite the flavorful dish she cooked, the film failed to generate much interest at the box office or enthusiastic response from the critics.

After *Water*, Mehta released *Heaven on Earth* (2008),[5] which told the story of an Indian woman tricked into an abusive marriage with an Indo-Canadian man. The film received cold shoulders from the critics and audience alike. Her latest film, *Midnight's Children* (2012), was an adaptation of the Booker Prize–winning novel of the same title by Salman Rushdie. Shot in Sri Lanka in more than a hundred locations, using eight hundred different actors and extras, it was perhaps the most ambitious film of her career. *Midnight's Children* was premiered at the Toronto International Film Festival in 2012 with great expectations, but the film failed to generate critical acclaim or box office success.

---

4. From the press kit for *Republic of Love*, p. 4.
5. The film was also released in India under the name *Videsh* (Foreign Country), dubbed in Hindi.

Methodology for Film Research

As the holder of a master's degree from one of the most reputed universities in India and a prospective candidate in its PhD program, Mehta attributes equal value to the rigor of academic research and the vigor of artistic endeavors. Throughout my interview, she reiterated her commitment to follow a clearly defined research methodology: "You have to study it academically," says Mehta. "You have to know where it starts, where it comes from, the social and cultural background. . . . It is important to start with the discipline of academia."

Similar to any academic research, Mehta's methodology starts with forming a research question:

> For me, it always starts with a question, says Mehta. I remember very distinctly, with *Fire* . . . saying something about women and choices, about the lack of them. . . . So the film came out of the question of extreme choice, and what is the fallout of that. . . . When I wrote *Water*, the environment was rampant with questions about the place of religion. . . . So it's always a question that starts my scripts. (Khorana 2009b: 2)

Once the question is conceived, she starts with a literature review, trying to read all the prominent scholars in the field of interest. Her primary source in the case of *Water* was Martha Chen, professor of sociology at Harvard University, who won a Padma Shri medal (a coveted honor given by the government of India to people who make outstanding contributions to the society) for her contribution to anthropological research in India. Chen's ethnographic study, published under the title *Perpetual Mourning: Widowhood in Rural India* (2000), provided a foundational framework for Mehta's screenplay. Mehta describes Chen as her "first window" into the world of widows and acknowledges that her research was a great source of inspiration as well as information.

The next step in the research process was a personal interview with Ginny Srivastava, a Canadian activist who runs an educational institution for widows in India, aptly named the Association of Strong Women Alone. Mehta remembers gratefully, "With Martha I had the whole sociological perspective, and with Ginny, insight into the[ir] practical [life]."

After completing the literature review and preliminary data sampling, Mehta embarked on a field research trip to Varanasi, Brindaban, and other cities along the banks of the River Ganges, where widow ashrams are situated. It was an active form of participant observation, immersing herself completely into the life of the widows and recording their individual and collective experiences.

Local informants provided valuable insights on the dynamics of the religious traditions of the context. She also collected other resources, such as photographs, artifacts, and archival records, all of which came in handy during the preproduction process.

When it comes to re-presentation of culture, Mehta takes advantage of film's artistic ability to convey information with minimum use of word or text. "It is the power of cinema," says Mehta. "A small movement can have powerful impact . . . the gesture of a hand, the wave of a lily pad, the way a frog jumps, the way Chuyia scratches her face, the curling of toes." Seemingly insignificant gestures of characters in a film can speak more loudly than volumes of ethnographic text. "When Chuyia asks, 'Where is the house for man-widows?'" according to Mehta, "the whole thesis of [Martha Chen's book] Perpetual Mourning is in there" (personal interview, June 12, 2013).

In all three films of the Elements Trilogy, the story is told from the perspective of a child protagonist. This is undoubtedly a testament to Mehta's attempt to maintain an objective viewpoint in dealing with social issues. A child is the embodiment of innocence, and in Mehta's own words, "they can ask questions the way the adults can't. . . . they aren't exposed to the world enough to know how to negotiate the meaning of things. It is very instinctive." This innocent eye is one of the most important qualities of an objective observer, and it is evident in every aspect, even in the movement of her camera. "I have an observing camera," says Mehta. "As opposed to an intrusive one." The camera is "motivated by the actors" and "triggered by the characters' action." It simply follows the actors, only seeing what they are seeing or doing. In the words of Hamilton, Mehta's producer, "She wants . . . to take the time to let the camera speak, to let the images speak for themselves" (Pungente 2005).

Even the selection of the color palette adds subtle nuances to the content of a frame: Fire uses a traditional red and yellow palette, Earth uses a natural earthy hue with a brown tint, and Water uses deep blue with a grayish white—all characteristics of the respective elements represented in each film.

In staging and acting decisions, Mehta considers Natyashastra, the Indian text on dramaturgy, her creative Bible. Compiled between the second century BCE and the second century CE, this text describes the various facial and bodily postures and expressions needed to perform the "nine basic emotions" of classical Indian dance-theater.[6] During the rehearsals, she lets the actors walk through a nine-block grid, exploring and expressing the nine emotions of *Natyashastra*.

The methodology adopted in film research may be quasi-scientific at best, yet it shows a healthy respect for the rigor of scholarly research. The inquiry of filmmakers into the cultural experiences of their characters at times reveals unanticipated and surprising insights into the ethnographic makeup of the diegetic world. Both artists and anthropologists struggle with the analytical and experiential sides of culture, trying to view it from the outside as an interpreter and from the inside as a participant. Ethnography attempts to engage readers' mind objectively, while film tries to engage viewers' heart subjectively.

Voice of Feminism

Mehta's films are often labeled as a megaphone for the voice of Indian feminism. The female protagonists in her films reflect an ideological stance on social issues, challenging the gender bias created by the patriarchal hegemony. In Mehta's own words, "It is [about] women against the patriarchal system and it is [about] religion being used to actually put down women. . . . It was the women who suffered the most because of the interpretation of Hinduism" (personal interview, June 12, 2013).

Indian feminism has a unique religious framework that stems from the concept of goddess worship in Hindu religion. Goddess is a ubiquitous myth in India, and the worship of female deities has been part of most Hindu sects. The goddess manifests in Indian culture as a caring mother, often called the mother goddess, who nurtures her devotees, or as a fierce avenger who retaliates for the evils committed against her devotees.[7]

Feminist critics in India have not always been sympathetic to

6. The eight original emotions are love, happiness, sadness (grief), anger, energy, fear, disgust, and surprise. A ninth emotion, peace or sublime tranquility (*shanta*), was added later. A wide variety of emotions are conveyed by facial and bodily gestures for the eyes, eyelids, eyebrows, nose, cheeks, lower lip, chin, mouth, and neck. There are also 67 gestures for the hands and many gestures for other parts of the body. *Natyashastra* is not a scientific study of the craft of acting, but rather a compilation of the stage experience of many actors.
7. Some feminists, however, find this religious connection unappealing. It is true that the women are treated as goddesses, but it also shuts them in a glass cage, merely as an object of worship, instead of considering them as equal partners in the culture-making process. Kathleen Erndl, for example, accuses the romantics of manipulating the goddess ideology to serve the interests of the patriarchal society and urges Indian feminists to "rescue 'Shakti' from her patriarchal prison" (2000: 17).

Mehta's portrayal of women in her films. Some consider her protagonists as hopeless victims of social conditions, not active fighters in the cause of social reformation. For example, Tejaswini Niranjana and Mary E. John comment:

> [*Fire*] ends up arguing that the successful assertion of sexual choice is not only a necessary but also a sufficient condition—indeed, the sole criterion—for the emancipation of women. Thus the patriarchal ideology of 'control' is first reduced to pure denial—as though such control did not also involve the production and amplification of sexuality—and is later simply inverted to produce the film's own vision of women's liberation as free sexual choice. (1999: 581)

Some critics express similar opinions about the women in *Water*. While the film succeeds in pointing fingers at the social crimes committed against women, Mehta conveniently forgets the equal and opposite force of rebellion initiated by women, "selectively obliterating the forms of protest emanating from the voices of educated widows" (Rai 2007: 211). As a result, "the progressive and thinking Indian women of the 1930s is sacrificed to put the submissive woman on a pedestal." The widows in the ashram could have embraced prostitution as a rightful means of survival, some would argue, instead of being forced into it by men. Even Shakunthala, perhaps the most feminist character of all, is imprisoned in a man's world. She confides all her rebellious thoughts to a male authority figure, the Pundit, and surrenders Chuyia into the hand of a man, either Narayan or Gandhi. Even for Kalyani, salvation could have come only through an alliance with Narayan. None of these women are feminist role models, the critics say, because they endure and suffer more than they fight, blindly professing submission to male authority figures in the name of faith.

Critics such as Madhuri Snigdha, in contrast, do not find this religious recourse problematic, because most social reform movements in India have had religious underpinnings. The Elements Trilogy is Mehta's way of responding to the dominance enacted on women in three different historical moments, in three different sociocultural locations, and in three different political contexts. The women of the trilogy may have been pushed to the margins of the society, but instead of being helpless victims, they create their own destiny. "Mehta depicts the ways in which the widows, especially Chuyia, Kalyani and Shakunthala, continuously intervene into the religious, cultural and social normative discourses," argues Snigdha, "and the ways in which they negotiate their economic oppression and resist their sexual domination within and outside of the Ashram" (Snigdha 2012, 50). In the same vein, Tutun Mukherjee also notes that the trilogy "addresses a global audience in an attempt to nudge the conscience of the success of feminism and the political reforms initiated by feministic ideology" (2007: 231).

Mehta does not take issue with critics on either side of the argument, because she is not interested in being put in a "feminist bracket." "I don't think of myself as a feminist filmmaker," says Mehta. "I would like to think of myself as someone who makes film that are humanitarian." She considers herself to be an advocate for anyone who fights for the freedom of conscience, irrespective of gender. For the same reason, she is skeptical of other labels attached to her films—for example, *Fire* being branded as an LGBT film. "*Fire* is not about lesbians," reiterates Mehta. "It is about the importance of emotional nurturing, and the deprivation that can happen in a patriarchal society" (personal interview, June 12, 2013). The homosexual relationship in the film is a metaphorical device she uses to expose the traditional framework of the Indian culture.[8] Though the same-sex issue raised the stakes for the film, for Mehta *Fire* is nothing more (or less) than about the emotional deprivation of women in a joint family system.

Hardly any female auteurs hold positions of creative control in Bollywood. The female role is relegated to the creation of erotic spectacle on the screen. As Virdi notes, "Women have no access to the means of film production and are still virtually unrepresented as directors, producers and screen writers. As actors they perform—directed by male fantasies and patriarchal values" (2003: 61). There have been many powerful actresses in Bollywood—Hema Malini, Nargis, and Shabana Azmi, to name a few—but they were merely "performers" whose job it is to execute the creative vision of the male directors. Bollywood does not nurture female participation in the creative process. The logistical problem with filmmaking is perhaps partly to blame. It is taboo for women to work late hours at night and to travel to difficult locations without being escorted by men. Ironically, the top three acclaimed

8. Even though there are no specific prohibitions against homosexuality in Hindu scriptures, orthodox Hindus allege that the portrayal of a homosexual relationship in *Fire* was abominable. Shiv Sena, one of the radical factions of Hinduism, described it as an "immoral and pornographic" film "against Indian tradition and culture." The same-sex relationship in the film was criticized as "not a part of Indian history or culture" and as "acts of perversion." A statement issued by Shiv Sena's women's wing said, "If women's physical needs get fulfilled through lesbian acts, the institution of marriage will collapse, reproduction of human beings will stop."

Indian filmmakers in the international scene today (Deepa Mehta, Meera Nair, and Gurindar Chaddah) are women of the Indian diaspora. A close examination of their careers indicates that their success can be attributed partially to the openness of the Western film industry: Canada for Deepa Mehta, the United States for Meera Nair, and the United Kingdom for Chaddah. "India gives me stories," says Mehta, "but it is Canada which gives me the freedom and opportunity to tell that story" (personal interview, June 12, 2013).

The Diasporic Gaze

The heart and soul of the Elements Trilogy lies in India, yet it is primarily a Canadian film series from the production perspective. The films are neither stereotypical art-house Canadian films nor the masala-style Bollywood films; they are an intelligent fusion of the two. Mehta's films, as Chaudhuri notes, have "enlarged the discursive boundaries of what can be represented in Indian cinema" (2009: 19), and therefore her filmmaking context can be considered "Bollywood with an extended boundary."

Mehta is a resident of Toronto, Ontario—a city often described as Hollywood North. It ranks third in the North American cities with the highest number of film productions, after Los Angeles and New York. The distinctively Canadian productions are mostly done in the Montreal-based French film market. Toronto- and Vancouver-based English productions unfortunately have to compete with Hollywood productions armed with bigger budgets and marketing networks.

Even though the film and television industry is thriving in Canada, Canadian films are little known even to Canadian audiences. Canadian talents tend to embrace Hollywood in order to get better media attention and more networking opportunities. Arguably the biggest name in Hollywood at present, James Cameron, who created the highest-grossing films in the history of the film industry—*Avatar* (2009) and *Titanic* (1997)—is a Canadian. Canada also has contributed popular actors (Jim Carrey, John Candy, Mike Myers, Ryan Gosling, Ryan Reynolds, Rachel McAdams) and dignified directors (Norman Jewison, David Cronenberg, Paul Haggis, Jason Reitman) to Hollywood. However, a number of homegrown auteurs such as Sarah Polly (*Away from Her*), Atom Egoyan (*Ararath*), and of course, Deepa Mehta, are not well known to the worldwide film community.

Apart from normal financing channels such as private investors, broadcasters, and distributors, Canadian producers heavily depend on funding from government agencies. The government of Canada regularly invests tax dollars to promote Canadian content in film and television productions. The National Film Board of Canada, established as part of a major legislative endeavor in 1939, produces documentaries and animation projects with little or no commercial orientation. In 1968, the Canadian Film and Development Corporation was established, primarily as a funding agency to provide tax shelter benefits for producers. The agency later changed its name to Telefilm Canada and is now active in funding productions with substantial Canadian content. Both federal and local governments provide nonreturnable tax credits for productions done within Canada. As a rule of thumb, a typical Canadian production has the potential to receive up to 20 percent of its production cost recovered in the form of tax credits.

According to David Hamilton, the producer of the trilogy, the Canadian government is very supportive of the industry, and organizations like Telefilm have a desire to help filmmakers. However, limited availability of funding makes the process highly competitive. Moreover, an important issue being debated is what makes a film (such as *Water*) Canadian, especially from the perspective of these funding agencies. Canadian content, for funding purposes, is measured by the degree of involvement of Canadian talents and production facilities in a film project. The subject matter is secondary and is not always the deciding criterion for funding eligibility. For the same reason, stories from different parts of the world and coproductions with other countries such as the United States, United Kingdom, Australia, and India is increasingly becoming common in the Canadian film industry.

Canada is a country that celebrates diversity, where multiculturalism is an official government policy. The government encourages immigrants from all over the world to celebrate their own cultural identity, encouraging the nation to find unity in diversity. In Hamilton's words,

> If we say we celebrate the peoples from all over the world . . . we must be a tomb to the kinds of stories and ideas and concepts that come with those people. It's not as if those peoples have corporal form and don't have any ideas in their heads, or don't have any history or don't have any family because they bring all these things with them. And of course, in bringing those things in with them, at least in the artistic world, they are going to want to express those things. (Pungente 2005)

Canadian films tend to be low-to-medium-budget productions with art-house style filmmaking, distributed mainly in the film festival route. The biggest problem Canadian producers face today is finding the proper distribution network for their films. U.S.-based companies consider Canada one of their domestic markets and own the distribution rights to Canada. It is practically impossible for Canadian films to break into the market unless a U.S.-based distributor acquires them. Therefore, Canadian filmmakers tend to follow the film festival route to get their films in front of the audience. The Toronto International Film Festival is one of the biggest festivals in North America, second only to the Sundance Film Festival. Also, other festivals such as the Vancouver Film Festival and the Atlantic Film Festival (Halifax) are increasingly becoming popular in the industry circle.

Fire was funded by independent investors who were in Mehta's personal circle. Half of the funds for *Earth* came from a private financier in India, and the other half came predominantly from the United States and United Kingdom. *Water* was funded primarily by Canadian sources, including government agencies such as Telefilm Canada. Since filmmaking is a budget-driven process, funding agencies often exercise unwarranted control over the production process. The investors try to influence the content of the film and use it as a venue for promoting their favorite causes and pushing their personal agendas. Mehta is very cautious of the dynamics between auteurs and their patrons in the filmmaking process. She is determined to keep her artistic integrity intact all the time, so she only works with the funding bodies that understand and appreciate the freedom she demands in the creative decision-making process. "Nobody dared to tell me 'do this' or 'do that.' . . . They know me," says Mehta. "I don't want a lawyer who is sitting in some fancy office to decide" whether Chuyia should get raped or not (personal interview, June 12, 2013).

Mehta looks at the culture through the eyes of a diasporic Indian. Therefore, her films need to be critiqued with a different set of interpretive lenses than is used for Bollywood. Her camera has a nostalgic gaze into the Indian culture, and her characters often struggling through a cultural identity crisis. Her protagonists are on a journey in search of a sense of belonging, whether in a family, in a nation, or in a religion. As a result, Mehta's films "resonate powerfully with Indian diaspora, often becoming their only connection with the homeland and the main intergeneration culture diasporic families share" (Virdi 2003: 2).

Mehta views herself as a cultural hybrid. Raised in India but living in Canada, she admits that she often felt "displaced": "I've never felt Canadian. I used to be upset about being called a visible minority. . . . I used to come to India and was called an NRI [Non Resident Indian] here. The problem was not about belonging anywhere; it was a dislike for labels" (Ramchandani 1998: 2). Mehta has repeatedly affirmed that she is not merely someone who visits India on holidays, but spends equal time between both her countries, and the social issues in India are as close to her heart as those in Canada. As one of Mehta's characters, Tom says to his friend Fay in *Republic of Love*, "Geography is destiny."

The diasporic stance tends to critique culture in negative terms or to exoticize it in order to market it for an international audience. In most cases, it creates cultural stereotypes that fit into the popular perceptions. Jasbir Jain suggests a fourth possibility, in which the people of the diaspora embrace a "living relationship" with the culture. When it happens, art serves as a "double mirror" where the "the outside sees us through them; we see ourselves in it in some kind of reflection" (2007b: x). The past is always present in the eyes of the diaspora, because history travels with an immigrant. Therefore, even though diasporic eyes can be extremely critical, they might also be able to "confer the strengths of a double vision, imparting a necessary critical distance" (Rai 2007: 202). This double vision is obvious in Mehta's films, as she explores the Indian culture from the vantage point of the West.

The diasporic eyes are viewed with suspicion by default. According to Rai, "Diasporic gaze is 'unidirectional' rather than 'interactive' stilling, and pacifying the agency of the subject" (2007: 204). Diasporic artists want to keep their ties to their country of origin while also trying to find acceptance in the new country, which results in "a duplication of uncritically examined attitudes of the country of new residence" (Singh 2007: 191). They assume a "privileged position" with funding from the first world, which in turn colors the credibility of their argument. Therefore, although diasporic voices project themselves as a voice of freedom, they can also be a "smokescreen" for commercial interest and marketing strategy.

Theories of diasporic gaze raise interesting concerns about the relationship between the ideology of art and culture. "Gaze" is not a neutral process of gathering information; it is, rather, "saturated with the residues of our social and cultural existence—for example, those relating to class, sexuality, economics" (Hawthorn 2006: 508). Stefania Basset observes that the way diasporic women construct their otherness in the art is "intertwined with the acknowledgement and bargaining of their identity as diasporic subjects" (2012: 8). Singh echoes the same sentiments as she notes "migration which gives rise to a diasporic population is also the crucible for a politics, which implicates both the new and the country of their origin" (2007: 191).

Sukhmani Khorana believes that diasporic identities need to be theorized and frames Mehta's works in the category of diasporic creativity as they "exemplify the creative diaspora's impulse to 'write/visualize back'" (2009a: 3).

The critics often accuse Mehta of portraying westernization and colonialism in a favorable light. In *Fire*, for example, the awakening comes through Sita, whose progressive thinking is signaled by the ways in which she wears pants, smokes cigarettes, and so on, which are typical symbols of Western culture. In *Water*, Narayan takes Kalyani on a quick tour of the British quarters, where he explains how differently (graciously) the Westerners treat their widows. The scene is well lit and the houses neatly organized, in contrast to the dark and gloomy portrayal of the ashram. In *Earth*, the British are the obvious villains, but the film often gives the impression that the colonialists were only doing them a favor by holding the many fighting factions of the subcontinent together as one nation. While Hindus, Muslims, and Sikhs are slaughtering each other, the only rational voice heard is that of the colonial power, without which the nation would fall apart. Mehta's position, some critics argue, is that the way Westerners treat the people is morally superior to that of the rest of the world, and the colonial rule of India was practically an act of benevolence. Vijay Singh, for example, comments, "As denizens of a 'post-colonial third world' one is forced by the contingent demands of contemporary global politics to view with suspicion all representations emerging from the 'first world' benevolence" (2007: 199).

Mehta's implication, they say, is that the indigenous societies would disintegrate without the supervision of colonial power. This is one of the reasons that Mehta's films are fiercely opposed in India. A group of critics describe her as "orientalist and neo-imperialist" and say her films should be rejected at face value. According to Rai, a "major portion of Mehta's gaze in *Water* are directed by the need to fulfill western needs for oriental fixities—the unchanging horror tale of a barbaric India" (2007: 208). The suffering of women in the non-Western world has always been the favorite topic of imperialists, who use it as a justification for the Western intervention in developing countries. According to Uma Mahadevan, "The portrayal of the colonial presence as a benevolent, civilizing mission ignores the very real effects of colonial oppression that led to the further impoverishment of Indian families, the brunt of which was borne by the women, especially the widows, in those families" (2007: 172).

Mehta's gratitude and appreciation toward the Western world have been obvious in my conversation with her. However, she nurtures no favoritism toward colonialism. *Earth*, for example, opens with a direct accusation of the colonial powers: "The arbitrary line of division the British would draw to carve up India in August 1947 would scar the subcontinent forever." She once described her films (particulary *Earth*) as an "exploration of what colonialism does to countries"—that "whenever they flew the country, they divided it. And they leave us holding the mess" (Craughwell 1999). Having said that, Mehta does not consider the West a demonic force that threatens the cultural aristocracy of India. According to her, the ultimate battle, to quote the Ice Candy Man in *Earth*, is against "the beast within us." If we keep blaming outside agencies instead of recognizing the demons that are really inside us, we will never be able to enjoy the ultimate freedom.

Summary

The stylistic sensibilities of the Elements Trilogy extend beyond the traditional boundaries of Indian or Canadian cinema and create a new category for our consideration: "Bollywood with extended boundaries" (Chaudhuri 2009: 19). As a filmmaker of the Indian diaspora, Mehta brings both etic and emic perspectives into the trilogy's representation of culture. As an insider, she sympathizes with the social actors and identifies with their struggles. As an outsider, she analyzes the root cause of these struggles and inspires the subjects to be agents of change and transformation.

In Mehta's own words, "The trilogy is about politics—*Fire* is about the politics of sexuality, *Earth* is about the politics of nationalism and *Water* is about the politics of religion" (Pungente 2005). The film series draws our attention to this threefold politics through a beautiful blend of fiction, image, and performance with an intensity that no other genre of ethnography can replicate.

It is safe to say that Mehta has exercised an anthropologist's precision in researching and re-presenting the culture, and the methodology she adopted is remarkably similar to that of the traditional methods in ethnographic research. Yet the trilogy also reflects Mehta's own personal search for identity. It is a journey through imagination, contemplation, and even meditation. The protagonists of the films travel the arc of this journey, and their collective search for meaning provides us the key to understanding the poignant sociocultural realities of India.

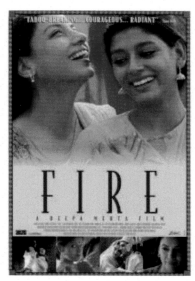

Fig. 5.1. DVD Cover for *Fire*; Mehta 1996

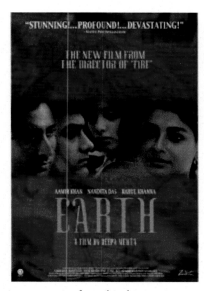

Fig. 5.2. DVD Cover for *Earth*; Mehta 1999

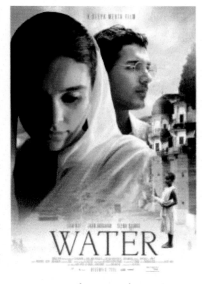

Fig. 5.3. DVD Cover for *Water*; Mehta 2005

Fig. 6.2. Varanasi: A view from the Ganges

Fig. 6.3. Tridents by the banks of Ganges

Fig. 6.4. The city of Gullies

Fig. 6.5. Funeral pyres along the Ganges

Fig. 6.6. Prescreening of *Water* in the widow ashram

Fig. 6.7. Screening of *Water* before focus groups

Fig. 6.8. Setting up for a focus group Indian style

Fig. 6.9. The author with Deepa Mehta

Fig 7.1. The Opening Shot of *Water*

Fig. 7.2a. The family in *Fire*

Fig. 7.2b. The family in *Earth*

Fig. 7.2c. The family in *Water*

Fig. 7.3. Pollution by the touch of a widow

Fig. 7.4. Gandhi as the hope for new nation in *Water*

Fig. 7.5a. Reenactment of the Agnipariksha in *Fire*

Fig. 7.5b. Reenactment of the Agnipariksha in *Fire*

Fig. 7.6. Narayan as the Krishna figure

Fig. 7.7. Holi and the Krishna symbolism in *Water*

6

———

Touching the Screen

Field Research in India

Cultural traditions that arise from religious thoughts and practices shape cinema in India.
—Gayatri Chatterji

In the previous chapter, we reviewed the Elements Trilogy from the perspective of its auteur and her filmmaking context. The cultural information depicted in the film is filtered through the lens of the filmmaker, who, like an anthropologist, suffers from a certain degree of reflexivity in her representation of culture. Therefore, what we receive from the film is ethnographic data of a secondary nature—an interpreted version of the actual data. In this chapter, we will attempt to verify the accuracy of Mehta's re-presentation of culture in the trilogy with specific focus on *Water*, by comparing it with the findings of my own field research in India. The research involves multiple methods in case study format, incorporating participant observation, focus groups, and interviews with local people, anthropologists, and the auteur herself.

A film generates complex and multivariable data, which can be studied more efficiently using a mixed-method approach. A case study does not solely depend on one specific method for data collection, but uses multiple methods, providing opportunities for triangulation. Information is drawn from multiple pieces of evidence to create a case study database with a broad spectrum of information—field notes, interview transcripts, personal journals, etc. (see fig. 6.1). In my research, the field data come predominantly from three sources: participant observation in Varanasi, focus groups conducted among viewers in India, and ethnographic interviews with local anthropologists and Deepa Mehta, the writer/director of the film.

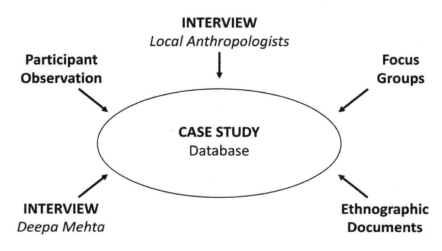

Fig. 6.1. *The Case Study's Multiple Sources of Evidence*

Focus groups are the industry standard for research on films and are widely used by the studios to analyze viewers' response. Ethnographic interviews rely on questions developed by the researchers and the administration of these questions to establish a consistency of response. In the case of participant observation, research is focused in the geographical context of the film in an attempt to establish the rationale for social actions and cultural behavior described in its diegetic world.

Participant Observation

I visited all three cities in which the story of the trilogy unfolds: New Delhi (*Fire*), Amritsar/ Lahore (*Earth*), and Varanasi (*Water*).[1] However, the primary research was carried out in Varanasi, the context of *Water*.

1. It is generally assumed that the fictional city Rawalpur, in which *Water* is set, is modeled after Varanasi.

It needs to be noted that although the filmic world of *Water* is India, the actual world we see on the screen is Sri Lanka. Mehta shot *Water* in Sri Lanka, fearing opposition from religious factions who sabotaged the initial shooting of the film in India. The artificial sets created in Sri Lanka, however, recreated Indian landscapes with scrupulous precision and provided authentic backdrops for the story of *Water*.

Situated on the banks of the holy river Ganges, Varanasi (according to Hindu mythology) is considered the holiest city in India (see fig. 6.2, gallery). Hindus believe that the waters of the Ganges can cleanse all sins accumulated in a lifetime. Lamb observes that "the flowing waters of the Ganges were thought to be potently freeing: placing the bones of the deceased in such waters was said to lead to the immediate release (*mukti*) of the soul from the world of *saṃsār*," notes Lamb. "It also brings peace (*śānti*) and well-being (*maṅgal*) to the soul" (Lamb 2000: 163). Therefore, it is common to see funeral services and ritual ablutions being performed on a continuous basis in the *ghats*—the embankments constructed along the river. The relationship between the sacred river and the city is the essence of Varanasi, and the river is often called *ma ganga* or the mother Ganges.

Varanasi is known as the spiritual capital of the country, crowded with countless temples and monasteries, attracting millions of pilgrims from all over the world. Often known by its British name, Banaras, it is also a center of literature, art, and culture. Banaras Hindu University (BHU), arguably the oldest university in India, is situated in this city. It is also popular for its handloom shops, which produce the famous Banaras silk, using a special weaving technique with silver and golden threads.

My site visit was arranged by the Sam Higginbottom Institute of Agriculture, Technology and Sciences (SHIATS), a local university situated in the nearby city of Allahabad. I enlisted a student social worker to act as my local informant. As a social worker who works closely with the indigenous people of Varanasi, he was familiar with local customs, traditions, and language.

When I arrived at Varanasi, I felt as if I were walking into one of the sets of *Water*. An excerpt from my field diary on the first day of my visit reads as follows:

As Mr. X told me, Varanasi is really a city of galleys [see fig. 6.4, gallery]. The streets are paved with stone, but are covered in mud and cow-dung. Some of the houses across the streets are turned into shady motels. As I walked, I kept bumping into children playing cricket or dogs swirling through mud. Little shops on both sides of the galleys sold sweets, spices, flowers and so on. It looked like a scene straight out of *Water* except for the pungent smell that gushed into my nose, almost knocking me unconscious." (Field Diary: 17)

One thing I noticed immediately was the "tridents" of different sizes and shapes planted on both sides of the Ganges, as they are portrayed in *Water* (see fig. 6.3, gallery). According to Indian mythology, Varanasi is believed to be resting on top of the god Shiva's trident. Idols of gods and goddesses are ceremonially worshipped in recesses along street corners, where people offered *prasad* (food sacrament) for their favorite deities.

The Ganges appeared muddy and brown, quite a contrast to the clear blue water depicted in the film. I noticed Save Ganga posters and graffiti on the riverbanks, urging immediate action from the government for the depollution of the river. The *Times of India*, the largest-circulation English newspaper in the country, notes that "the sacred river is black and huge methane bubbles constantly burst onto the surface. The fecal coliform level is more than 3,000 times the permissible level" (Varadarajan 2000: 212).

I visited many *ghats* along the Ganges, the most popular being the Aasi Ghat. When I arrived at the *ghat*, a film shoot was in progress:

Wandering Sadhus [Hindu monks] were taking a bath in the river. A group of children were scavenging for recyclables in the garbage pile. A band of tourists, a few of them westerners, were smoking Ganja under a tree. A *satsang,* "community meeting," was being held under another tree. A group of villagers were engaged in animated conversations with local politicians. Some of them were distracted by a film shooting, which was progressing on the other side of the *ghat*. A big crowd had gathered around the film crew. They were particularly curious because the lead actor seemed to be a white woman. A flock of menacing cows kept interrupting the shoot as they wandered fearlessly into the set. (Field Diary: 32)

I also witnessed the funeral ceremonies being performed on a continuous basis along the *ghats* (see fig. 6.5, gallery). The relatives of the diseased carried the dead bodies to the funeral pyre in bamboo stretchers, and as they patiently waited until the bodies were burnt, they smoked cigarettes or chewed pan. They sometimes negotiated, often vociferously, with street vendors who were selling firewood for cremation. Those who could not afford sufficient firewood did not hesitate to dump the partially burnt bodies into the river. According to my informant, the bodies of pregnant women, sadhus, and children were not burnt; they were rather simply floated in the water.

Apart from conversing with local people and focus group members, I also had an unexpected opportunity to spend a day in a widow ashram run by a Christian mission organization (fig. 6.6, gallery). The ashram was inside a two-story building, where the widows operated a bakery and a tailor shop, which generated partial income for their sustenance. Eight widows lived in the institution, all of them disowned by their own respective families. They were either referred to the ashram by local missionaries or rescued from the streets by social workers.

My visit was under the supervision of the head widow (matron) and a caretaker, who functioned as the administrator. I couldn't help but notice that the head widow had thick, long hair and wore a colorful sari, unlike the widows in *Water*. Out of the eight widows in the ashram, only two had short hair. All of them were clad in pale-colored saris, while a young widow wore a *churidar*. They spoke Hindi with a local slang, which made it difficult for me to understand. An Australian missionary, fluent in both English and Hindi, acted as an interpreter. Mostly the matron and the caretaker spoke on behalf of the others. As much as the widows looked happy and content, the stories they shared were dark and depressing, but deeply moving. Here is an excerpt from one of them:

> My son is a lawyer. I had been a widow since he was a teenager. But everything changed when he got married. His wife did not like me and always tried to find fault with me. She also insisted that I should sign my husband's property over to them so that they could apply for a bank loan. She abused me almost every day, both physically and mentally. She even made me starve many days. My son did not have the courage to say anything. Last year they took me to Kashi [another name for Varanasi] for the Kumbha Mela festival. After the ceremonies, they dropped me off at the temple and said "this is your new home" and then they drove away. They did not give me money to buy food or even arrange a place for me to stay. I slept under a tree and begged for food to survive. (Field Diary: 42)

All the widows commented that they really "liked" the film. They attested that the social stigma against the widows portrayed in the film is "not at all exaggerated" and that widows still suffer the same degree of deprivation, especially in rural areas. However, they were also quick to comment that the life in their ashram is very different from what is portrayed in the film. "It is different for us here," one of the widows said. "This is like a family. It is fun. We would rather be here than in our own homes."

After having spent nearly three months in Varanasi, I came to appreciate the precision with which Mehta recreated the cultural landscape of the city for *Water*. She has painted the chaotic life of widows in Varanasi with an elegant artistic brush, making the city both revolting and captivating at the same time. Of course, she has exploited the privileges of dramatic license in the process, but it does not seem to have affected the rendition of social issues in the film.

Focus Groups

I conducted five focus groups in Varanasi, three of which were organized at Banaras Hindu University (BHU) in the residence of one of their faculty members. Nearly half of the participants were invited guests from outside the campus, while the others were either students or faculty of the university. Three other groups were held at the SHIATS campus. Professors from the anthropology, film studies, and religious studies departments of SHIATS showed keen interest in promoting the research project. The institute also provided all logistical support necessary for administering the groups.

At first, the movie was screened for invited guests in the auditorium (see fig. 6.7, gallery). The viewers were then split into three different focus groups to meet at various time slots (see fig. 6.8, gallery). Each group had a combination of participants from various academic, economic, and social backgrounds, but most of them were students or faculty connected to the university.

I formed a topic guide based on the informal discussions I had with my informant. Instead of preparing a questionnaire, I converted the questions into sample themes on social issues and asked the group what they thought about the way in which the film deals with these issues. The questions were posed flexibly by providing a range of alternative choices to which members could choose to respond individually or as a group. The primary focus of my role as the moderator was to ensure that a "collective sense is made, meaning negotiated and identities elaborated through the process of social interaction between people" (Wilkinson 1999, quoted in Barbour 2007: 26).

The dynamics of social interactions in a group are an important component of data analysis. Conflicting opinions were rare; the participants almost always agreed with each other without much debate. One of the weaknesses of the focus group method is the probability of a dominant member controlling the opinion of the group. Some movie enthusiasts kept deflecting the conversations into topics related to technical aspects of filmmaking, but I tactfully brought back the conversation to the objectives of the research. In the end, I realized that, as Bernard notes, a moderator requires "the combined skills of an ethnographer, a survey researcher, and a therapist" (2006: 237).

I also noticed the effect of gender difference in participation: The male participants tended to discredited Mehta's outlook on social issues at face value, arguing that her lens was tainted with feminist prerogatives. The female participants, in contrast, seemed to have strong agreement with Mehta on the deeper concerns expressed in the film. They offered more insightful criticism, with their comments focusing on the central theme of the film—the suffering of the widows.

All groups consisted of people from different religious backgrounds, and it was interesting to observe the biases and cultural assumptions that subtly influenced their comments. People of different religious upbringings perceived the key topic of discussion, deprivation of widows, differently. For example, Christians and Muslims focused more on the physical suffering of the widows, while Hindus focused more on the issue of oppression, mental affliction, and other forms of psychological suffering.

Interviews

Two local anthropologists graciously volunteered their time to meet with me and discuss their take on the social issues raised in *Water*. I used the insights gained from the focus groups to formulate the questions for my interviews, both of which were conducted at SHIATS.

One of them is an accomplished scholar with a master's degree in sociology and a doctorate in anthropology from Allahabad University. She is Muslim by birth but an active member of the BJP (Bharatiya Janata Party), a political party deeply rooted in conservative Hindu ideologies. Further, she teaches in a university run under Christian management. She describes herself as a "secularized" citizen of India who respects and appreciates all religious viewpoints.

The second interviewee is a research assistant in the department of anthropology at SHIATS. Originally from Brazil, she moved to India to do postdoctoral research on the role of cultural taboos among Indian women on issues related to health care and medicine. She considers herself to be in an ideal position as an ethnographer because, in her own words, "I can wear my Indian glasses anytime to get a subjective experience of being with the women. I can also take it out anytime and observe them from an objective point of view" (personal interview, June 7, 2013). She also happens to be an avid fan of Bollywood films, including the Elements Trilogy, which she regards as valuable ethnographic documents in the study of Indian culture.

Filmmakers are not easily accessible to the general public and are not usually interested in academic discourses. However, Deepa Mehta, the writer and director of the Elements Trilogy, was a pleasant exception (see fig. 6.9, gallery). As I approached her for an interview, Mehta tried her best to fit me into her already busy schedule. I still had to wait for almost another year to meet with her, as the production of her other films often got in the way.

I drafted a series of semistructured questions and sent it to her two weeks in advance so that she would have enough time to prepare for the interview. I drafted these questions based on the available data gathered from my field research in India.

As a filmmaker of the Indian diaspora, Mehta brings both etic and emic perspectives to her interpretation of Indian culture. As an Indo-Canadian myself, I could personally identify with this double consciousness; my reflexivity as a diaspora Indian turned out to be an advantage that helped negotiate and appreciate the meaning conveyed in the trilogy from the perspective of its auteur.

Ethnographic Documents

I was also able to locate a number of ethnographic reports that deal with the life of widows in India, authored by both Indian and Western anthropologists. Of particular interest, *Widows, Renunciation, and Social-Self: A Study of Bengali Widows in Varanasi* (2009) by Bandana Majumdar provides a comprehensive analysis of both material and nonmaterial deprivation faced by the widows in India. The book is a product of Bandana's rigorous research among 250 Bengali widows living in the city of Varanasi, who were interviewed extensively on the intensity of their deprivation, renunciation, and the formation of a social-self. I used these documents to draw insights to corroborate the data and substantiate the validity of my findings.

Ethnographic Analysis

It is to be noted that my study took place soon after the notorious Delhi rape case,[2] which created an international outcry against the way women are being treated in India. I could sense an overall tone of remorse and guilt in their response, and a suspicion that the Western media would caricature all Indian men as Eve teasers (sexual harassers) and abusers. "I am an Indian. Every bit of it," one of the participants proudly affirmed. "[Therefore] my blood boils when I see this. I feel embarrassed, especially when Western people see this."

The reflexivity of the participants manifested particularly in their preconceived bias against the filmmaker. Their emotional response to the film was often scathing, if not hostile. They used words like *hurt* and *disgusted* multiple times to describe what they felt while watching the film. They felt "hurt" by the blanket accusation of Indians as perpetrators of social evils, "exploited" by being exoticized for Western audiences, "disgusted" by Mehta's effort to promote a film by intentionally engaging in controversies, and "uncomfortable" about the outside world's perception of India.

I also observed an attitude of prejudice among the local Indians against the Indians of the diaspora. Uma Parameswaran talks about the "overt and covert antagonism that toxicise the communications between Indians in India, and NRIs" (2007: 10). The diasporic Indians, the locals suggest, tend to capitalize on Indian culture by exoticizing it for the international audience. Mehta, being one of them, exaggerates reality to emotionally manipulate the viewers, especially those in the West. "She is closely following the success of Salman Rushdie," a focus group member argued. "Controversy sells." As more indigenous auteurs are following the path of diaspora filmmakers like Mehta, the portrayal of culture, especially religious aspects of the culture, is increasingly becoming cynical and accusatory. As Vasudev observes, "Blind, superstitious belief as part of an ancient tradition are unscrupulously fostered as a way of keeping the ignorant permanently acquiescent, is a theme being tackled by number of filmmakers" (1986: 61). Some participants even claimed that they would rather trust the interpretation of their culture by non-Indian filmmakers such as Ang Lee (*Life of Pi*, 2012) or Richard Attenborough (*Gandhi*, 1986), who in

---

2. A young girl nicknamed Nirbhaya (Fearless) was gang-raped and killed by a group of men in a private bus on December 16, 2012. (Harris 2013).

their opinion possess a more objective eye than diaspora filmmakers like Mehta.

The participants approached *Water* first on a film qua film basis, critiquing its cinematic language and aesthetic qualities before entering into ideological discussions. The most recurring themes are listed in table 6.1 based on their frequency of occurrence in the discussions.

Table 6.1

Film Aesthetics: Recurring Themes

Serial Number	Theme
1	Mix of art-house and parallel cinema
2	Romanticism in a Bollywood mold
3	Scenes too perfect and too beautiful to be considered "real"
4	Visuals dim and colorless from a Bollywood perspective
5	A blend of ethno-music and Bollywood beats

As the table indicates, the film did not fit into participants' conventional understanding of movie genre. On the one hand, *Water* appeared to be a "thesis" film with an explicit social agenda, using an art-house style storytelling method, typical to Canadian films. At the same time, it also incorporates the stylistic sensibilities of Bollywood with its masala-style fusion of various genres. For some critics, for example, the film looked "too staged" and "too contrived" for them to feel its social criticism was "realistic" or "serious." The beauty of the landscapes and the misery of the widows offered a perennial contrast throughout the film, but many critics thought Mehta's obsession for aesthetic appeal robbed the scenes "from the ground of reality" (Jodha 2007: 51).[3] The visual style certainly augmented the entertainment value, which is a defining characteristic of Bollywood films. At the same time, the plot was too dark, and the pacing too slow, for it to be considered a film of the traditional Bollywood mold. Mehta attributes this style to a deliberate stylistic choice she made: "We wanted the frames to be beautiful because the condition of these women were so filled with despair," says Mehta. She adds that she wanted to contrast "the beauty of the world

3. As a general rule, neorealist films consider aesthetic appeal as a "cinematic impurity." Satyajit Ray once said, "I should also like to banish from my films every last trace of the theatrical and even the pictorial or prettified—two of the most common cinematic impurities" (Jodha 2007: 50).

and the despair within it or vice versa" (personal interview, June 12, 2013).

Water's confrontation of cultural taboos generated mixed responses from the participants. While portrayal of the customs and traditions could be true to its time period (1930s), they argued that the same assumptions are not valid for the society today. The participants were reluctant to admit that the widows are forced to live outside their family home with no option but to beg or prostitute for their livelihood. The existence of such brutal customs in pre-independence India was mostly a mistake of the past, which has no relevance in Indian society today. Now, since widows are legally allowed to remarry, widow ashrams, according to majority opinion, are nothing but relics of the past.

A number of ethnographic documents reveal the fact that Mehta has exercised an ethnographer's sensitivity in re-presenting the ceremonial aspects of culture, especially those associated with widowhood. Shankar et al. describe the actual rituals in a remarkably similar way as portrayed in *Water*: "A widow was disfigured by removing hair and was made to look ugly. She had to wear simple white or black saree." (2004: 155). Lamb also describes this ritual among the widows in the Maghalian tribe of West Bengal: "As her husband's body is taken by men to be burned, women take her to the pond, where they break her bangles, wash the red powder out of her hair, and robe her in a white sari. She will never again wear the ornaments and beautiful saris of a *suhagin*, but instead will live a life of asceticism in her dead husband's household." (Heinz 1999) According to Ramanamma and Chaudhari, "The dress code at widowhood is also introduced in a horrifying manner—by breaking the bangles with a stone." They also note that the "widows have to survive on a simple diet, often unhealthy diet, and hence many a times they die of malnutrition" and are "further humiliated by tonsuring their heads" (2004: 122). Bandana Majumdar's research portrays the everyday life of the widows in strikingly similar details: "Wrapped in a single white sari, they were to survive on a single small vegetarian meal a day, being confined to a specified portion of the house, and spending almost all their time in worshipping gods and goddesses of the Hindu pantheon. Even their physical presence on certain auspicious occasions was considered inauspicious" (2009: 78). Martha Chen also describes her meeting with a widow in a similar tone: "Her head was shaved, she was dressed in a white sari, her bangles were broken and the red dot (*pottu*) on her forehead was removed.

Since then the only place she has gone to is the temple. She has not been allowed to attend any weddings, even those that took place in her own house" (2000: 115).

There are direct religious connotations to these cultural taboos as well. Patil observes, "A widow is feared and imagined as a bad omen. Of the eight incarnations of the Devi in Hindu mythology, the most feared is 'Dhumavati' in the form of a widow accompanied by the raven as her vehicle" (Mukherjee 2007: 220). Ramanamma and Chaudhari in the same vein note that married women are instructed to avoid any direct contact with widows, because they are considered to be "the earthly incarnation of 'Alakshmi', the personification of evil luck and misfortune" (2004: 121).

Majumdar confirms the existence of child widows in Varanasi. Though child marriage is legally banned in India, sixty-four widows she met were under the age of nineteen, and four of them were under nine years old. Almost half of the subjects (approximately 42 percent) were young widows under thirty. Their deprivation was heightened by the meaninglessness of their existence, as they are unable to contribute to the society even though they possessed necessary qualifications and experience. Therefore, "both material and non material or emotional deprivations were intertwined" in the life of the widows.[4]

Water is footnoted with a postscript that reads, "There are over 34 million widows in India, according to the 2001 census. Many continue to live in social, economic and cultural deprivation as prescribed 2000 years ago by the Sacred Texts of Manu." The statistics cannot be disputed, of course, but the postscript virtually fast-forwards the narrative of the film all the way to the present day, implying that India is still governed by the rules of Manu. The participants particularly took offense at this comment because it suggests that nothing much has changed since the 1930s.[5] Even though Mehta does not overtly state this, she clearly gives the impression that the widows are treated the same way in India today as they were over a hundred years ago. This is an attempt "to project an India in a frozen time-warp" (Singh 2007: 198) and to throw the Indian culture into the "sociological prison of

---

4. As a result, Majumdar identifies a "formation of selfhood," which is described as "an attribute, or property of a person being self-centered, contrary to the formation of social-self, which is a socio-centric property of a person who is actively engaged in performing various types of socially productive roles" (Majumdar 2009: 229).
5. On the contrary, the recent statistics released by the government of India (Census 2011) indicate that there is a "massive spike in the number of widows in India." The percentage of those widowed increased from 0.7 percent of the population in the 1930s to 4.6 percent in 2011 (TNN: 2015).

the diasporic gaze," which has a "predilection to engage with the construction of an unchanging India—mythical and exotic in reimagining
and reinterpreting the past" (Rai 2007: 214–15). One of the focus group
participants asked, "What if a movie is made on racism in America in
a particular year which ends with 'x number of Americans still experience racism today?' What would you feel?"

Artistic rendition of the history of a nation shapes the imagination
of its future generations. This is what elevates the role of an artist to
that of a social reformer. Mehta assumes this responsibility as *Water*
"exposes the historical and contemporary vulnerability of the Indian
people," admits Jodha. "But she forgets to establish their ability to
resist and fight back" (Jodha 2007: 47). Most participants felt that
Mehta should have made an attempt to acknowledge the social changes
that have taken place in India since its independence through enlightened Indians like Narayan.

Table 6.2

Film's Cultural Authenticity

Serial Number	Film's Authenticity
1	Mehta has a hidden agenda.
2	Film tries to reinforce the stereotypical understanding of the male-female relationship.
3	Film misuses dramatic license to exaggerate reality.
4	Film inappropriately attacks Hinduism.
5	Film promotes Western values.
6	Film tries to exoticize Indian culture.
7	Film tries to create hype to grab attention.

The participants argued that Mehta deliberately attempts to stereo-
type the Indian culture, especially the male-female relationship in
social interactions (see table 6.2). Instead of explicating social issues
in their context, she uses them as devices that reinforce cultural type-
casts forged by Western sociologists. "Filmmakers try to capitalize on
the quirkiness of our culture," one of the focus group members com-
plained. "[Diasporic] Indians come to India, share our story and tell
everyone how bad we are. . . . Look at the way they treat their women,
and they make money out of it. These people exploit our culture."

Mehta's art is "choreographed by her allegiance to specific polemical concerns or ideas and their marketability," argues Jodha. "Mehta's advocacy of a 'cause' and her reformist zeal is a smokescreen that has strong commercial and media appeal, but beyond it her inheritance of India is an inheritance of loss and depravity" (Jodha 2007: 52).

This anxiety of "cultural self-image" often propelled the participants to denigrate any proposition that would characterize men's attitude toward women in a bad light. There was a general tendency to downplay the severity of social issues presented in the film, arguing that the oppression of women is more of a universal problem than a context-specific issue in India. One participant lauded India's position on diversity, pointing out that the Americans who will watch the movie and consider India to be backward and discriminatory "should think about how a nation with a Hindu majority sees a Roman Catholic woman [Sonia Gandhi] elected as the prime minister, only to give her seat to a Sikh man, who was sworn in by a Muslim president." A few, however, were bold enough to admit that the issues discussed in the film are pertinent social realities that need to be addressed and remedied. According to a local anthropologist, "What Mehta has shown is a social reality. Obviously people want to hide it under the rugs and let no one know about it. . . . If we are ashamed of it, we should rather strive to eradicate it" (personal interview, June 6, 2013).

Even those who belong to other religious traditions felt that Mehta unfairly targets Hinduism as the root cause of all social evils in India (see table 6.3). "Hindus are too gentle or too scared to protest the way the Muslims do," a focus group member commented. "So anybody can take unfair liberties with Hinduism." It is true that certain social classes in India treat women, particularly the widows, poorly, but this has nothing to do with religion. One participant said, "I've no doubt one could live the life of a devout Hindu without believing that widows are responsible for their husband's deaths."

Some participants drew attention to the idea that women are treated like goddesses in Hinduism, a concept regarded blasphemous in many other religious traditions. Many families in India are governed by matriarchs, widows or not, who enjoy inscrutable authority. Even Mehta herself admits in her interview that she comes from one such family: her grandmother, who was a widow, continued to stay in the family house after her husband's death and enjoyed privileged status as the family matriarch.

Table 6.3

Religious Endorsement of Oppression

Serial Number	Religious (Hindu) Endorsement of Oppression
1	The oppressors don't know the "true spirit" of Hinduism.
2	The scripture quoted in the film (Manu-smriti) is outdated.
3	True Hinduism treats women as goddesses.
4	Oppression is more of a social issue than a religious issue.
5	Oppression is caused by superstitions in folk Hinduism.

A general consensus emerged among the participants that those who oppress women in the name of religion do not know the true spirit of religion. It is always the power-hungry leaders on top of the hierarchy who exploit religion by manipulating the believers. What needs to change is the mind-set of the people, not the tenets of religion themselves. As one participant suggested, "It is our egos that lead to misinterpretation of the scriptures."

In my observation, deprivation of widows still prevails in India. The root cause of this social evil, however, as Mehta seems to indicate, is not religion, but economics. Participants wholeheartedly conformed to Narayan's point of view in the film: "It is not religion; it is just about money." One participant said, "They [widows] are treated badly because they have basically nothing to give out. It starts from within your own family. So now you find a person is suddenly becoming a liability." Widows are forced to live in the ashram because their families want to repossess the wealth these women legally inherited from their diseased husbands. By getting rid of a widow from the household, as Narayan says, the family saves "one mouth to feed, four saris, one bed and a corner in the family home." In other words, the deprivation that the widows suffer in India, in reality, is an economic problem disguised as an oppressive religious tradition. The government initiatives in the field of education have helped alleviate this problem to some extent, and the country has made tremendous progress in this area from where it was in the 1930s. However, widows still suffer similar deprivation and cultural stigma, especially in the rural parts of India.

Summary

Cinema embodies the cultural experiences of one community, which are shared within the context of another (viewing) community. As an inherently subjective medium, film is susceptible to different readings by different viewers, and its portrayal of cultural information is open to individual interpretation. One would like to think that film has an intrinsic value, but in reality, there is always an ideology attached to it, if not by the filmmakers, then at least by the viewers. The meaning of a film, therefore, exists in this relationship between producer's intent and audience response, both of which bring their own ideologies into the hermeneutic cycle.

The field research presented in this chapter shows that the methodology used for cultural exegesis of film will be able to map the transaction of meaning between filmmakers and viewers to a reasonable degree of accuracy. Authentic portrayal of ethnographic information in *Water* helped viewers participate in the lived reality of its diegetic world. Though none of the participants were alive in the 1930s, the film enabled them to virtually travel back in time and space to share the lived reality of the characters. "I learned something new about my own culture," a participant commented with enthusiasm. "There are many customs in my own world I am not aware of!" When the researcher virtually enters into the diegetic world of a film in this manner, and participates in the story, it functions as a datum of culture.

7

Crisis of Faith

A Religious dialogue with the Elements Trilogy

The message [of the Elements Trilogy] is very particular to a certain point, but it is also universal in a totally different way.... How religion is misinterpreted for one's personal gain ... is true in every major religion. I'm sure you could say the same thing about Christianity, or Islam, or Buddhism. Crisis of faith is universal.
—Deepa Mehta

Water opens with a wide shot of an algae-infested pond, sprinkled with exquisite lotus flowers (see fig. 7.1, gallery). While the expanse of water clues us into the title of the film, lotus flowers set the religious undertone of the plot. Indian audiences immediately recognize the lotus flower as the ubiquitous symbol of an enlightened mind.

For others, this symbolism is revealed later in the film: "Lotus is untouched by the filthy water it grows in," says Kalyani. "Not everyone can live like a lotus flower," responds Narayan.

This opening is our invitation to enter into a world allegorical to that of the pond—a sisterhood of women, striving to survive in a world tainted by cultural taboos and social stigmas against their very existence.

This religious symbolism is further accentuated by the fact that the story takes place on the banks of the Ganges, the holy river of India.

The Ganges is considered to be the virtuous mother of humanity, often described as *Ma Ganga* (Mother Ganges). According to Nitin Kumar, "Ganga's heavenly origin and descent to the earth makes her an effective intermediary between the two worlds, a continuous, ever flowing link between the two realms" (Kumar 2003).

Cinematic and cultural symbols are intertwined in the diegetic world of the trilogy, but we will be interested primarily in the religious themes emerging from its visual narrative. We focus our religious criticism primarily on *Water*, because it is described by Mehta as a portrayal of "the politics of religion."

The Politics of Religion

In India, religious sentiments are not relegated to private life; they are rather shared and celebrated in the public sphere. Therefore politics and religion are integrally connected in Indian culture. A classic example of this connection is the concept of *Ramarajya* (the kingdom of God), a term coined by Gandhi, which is frequently used in Indian politics even today. It is a term borrowed from the *Ramayana* and it represents the kingdom established by the god Rama—an ideal nation under the rule of God, characterized by peace and prosperity.

In *Earth,* the spirit of nationalism is at a delicate balance between religious ideologies in the community of local men gathered in the Lahore market. This group of men represents how the nation itself functions as a family, despite all social, economic, and religious diversities. Their religiosity is based on the shared experience of community and the brotherhood of humanity. As Husain reminds, "We share the same food, same language, and the same enemy."

We witness the tragedy of the unholy alliance between politics and religion when these men turn against each other like a close-knit family being torn apart. Religion becomes a divisive factor on the day of independence, when religious affiliation begins to define one's national identity. India, like Lenny's broken plate, was broken into pieces with no possibility for reconciliation. Santha becomes a symbol of the beaten, bruised, and raped nation torn apart in the clash between national integration and religious dissonance.

Water also redefines the boundaries of what is perceived as "family" in traditional Indian culture. The widows are rejected by their own families, but this alienation becomes the basis of their kinship. "In grief we are all sisters here," says Madhumati. "This house is our only refuge." In the outside world, these women would have had different social status with little or no chance of interaction, but inside the ashram, they are part of the same family. The ashram, like the nation, is meant to be a sisterhood—a community of fellow-sufferers. However, it has become a despicable ghetto, characterized by deprivation and corruption. The crumbling roof and peeling walls of the ashram thus become symbols of the skeletons of the nation's archaic past.

In this portrayal of nation as a family, we see one of the unique traits of Bollywood films we already discussed in chapter 4: film tends to portray "family as the primary trope to negotiate caste, class, community, and gender divisions ... through which it configures the nation and constructs a nationalist imaginary" (Virdi 2003: 7). Family is the prototype of society; all events happening within a family circle represent the social events taking place in the wider society.

"Family in many ways is the subject of all my films," says Mehta (see figs. 7.2a–c, gallery). "The house of widows in *Water* and the gathering in the marketplace in *Earth*. That is their family" (personal interview, June 12, 2013). For Mehta, true kinship emerges out of shared experiences in a community, like that of the ashram in *Water* or the group of friends in *Earth*. Family is not merely a network of individuals interconnected through blood relationships, but a social organism that creates a communal bond between different members of society.

What further divides the family is the unbridgeable gap between people of the different castes.[1] Madhumati describes the old auntie as "lucky" because "Brahmin widows" are keeping vigil for her body. The auntie, being a lower-caste woman, would otherwise have had no association with an upper-caste woman like Madhumati. In the romantic subplot of *Water*, Narayan is a Brahmin, who is at the top of the caste pyramid, and Kalyani, simply by being a widow, is at the very bottom. According to Manu-smriti, any physical intimacy between them is both formidable and forbidden. If an offspring were born out of their relationship, it would have been considered a "living dead." According to Manu-smriti, "The son whom a Brahmana begets through lust on a Sudra female is, (though) alive (*parayan*), a corpse (*sava*), and hence

---

1. Since ancient times, Hindus have held a view that people function differently in society in accordance with the order of their birth. The Hindu caste system divides people into four basic castes and one outcast group. The four main religious classes are Brahmins (priests), Kshatriyas (warriors), Vaisyas (traders/farmers), and Sudras (servants). The outcastes, called Dalits (once referred to as Untouchables), are the lowest in the social order. A person belongs to a particular caste purely based on heredity. There is no possibility to cross over from one caste to another based on individual merits.

called a Parasava (a living corpse)" (Manu-smriti 9.178), and "A Brahmana who takes a Sudra wife to his bed, will (after death) sink into hell; if he begets a child by her, he will lose the rank of a Brahmana" (Manu-smriti 3.17).[2]

The social stratification enforced through the caste system is maintained by the concept of "ritual pollution" carefully woven into the social fabric of India. The fear of pollution is one of the main reasons that people from one caste do not associate with people of other castes. According to Dhavamony, "The theory and practice of pollution assumed such great proportion so that the touch and even the sight of the untouchables was considered to be polluting" (Dhavamony 2002: 173). Untouchables are believed to pollute anyone who comes in direct contact with them. When a woman who has just finished taking a bath accidentally bumps into Kalyani, she furiously returns to the river to wash away the impurity caused by a widow's touch (see fig. 7.3, gallery). As Ramanamma and Chaudhari note, "An upper caste Hindu will purify himself with an ablution if the first person to cross his way is a widow" (2004: 121).

Social deprivation of widows, the main issue being discussed in *Water*, was literally a "burning" issue in India at the time. The notorious custom of *sati* (the burning of widows on the funeral pyre of their dead husbands) was a tradition endorsed and encouraged by religious texts. As Datta observes, this custom was indicative of the "degeneracy of religion into cruel superstition and prejudice of priesthood and family members into wily agents of death" (1998: 219). The great philosopher and political activist Raja Ram Mohan Ray, whose contribution is alluded to in the film, successfully persuaded the British government to legally prohibit *sati*. But the custom eventually transformed itself into a form of psychological torture wherein the widows were condemned to a life of renunciation that was worse than the physical burning.

Mehta's camera closes in on Chuyia as she goes through the ritualistic denigration of a widow, as she is stripped off the privileges of marital bliss. According to Pundit, when a woman becomes a widow, she has only three options: "They can burn with their dead husbands, or lead a life of self-denial, or if the family permits, marry their husbands' younger brother." A widow is considered socially dead, and her presence inauspicious in a public place. The family takes her away from

2. Manu-smriti texts are available at https://www.scribd.com/doc/7189037/Manu-Smriti-Sanskrit-Text-With-English-Translation.

the funeral pyre of her husband to the dark of night, where they break her bangles, wipe off her *tilak*, and shave her head. She is forced to renounce all adornments, cosmetics, and even eating sweets or fried food. In the end, she is dressed up in a white sari and sent off to an ashram.

Mehta captures many taboos associated with widowhood though an assortment of scenes. When Shakunthala draws water from the river, the priest who is officiating a wedding ceremony issues a stern warning: "Watch it. Don't let your shadow touch the bride." As Chuyia runs after the dog, Kalyani reminds her, "Widows are not supposed to run in public." As the love-struck Narayan follows Kalyani to the ashram, she politely reminds him, "It is a sin to follow a widow." When Chuyia chuckles over a silly joke, Kalyani reproves her: "[Widows] are not supposed to laugh in public."

The widows are mandated by the traditions to suppress the zest for life, their sexual desires in particular. "If widows start to fantasize, they will become blind," says Kalyani. Shakunthala is afraid of losing her constant battle with the flesh even after meticulously observing all prescriptions of ascetic piety. When Punditji asks her, "Do you feel any closer to self-liberation?" her honest response is, "If it means detachment from worldly desires, then no."

Although Narayan says, "It is not religion; it is just about money," it is very clear that the social evil is sustained through religious endorsement. Both religion and economics are partners in crime and are equally guilty. As Mehta puts it, "It is a religion being used to actually put down women but not in the sense to just put down women but basically for economics, which is everything, you know. Money makes the world go round, sadly enough. These were women who suffered the most because of the interpretation of Hinduism" (personal interview, June 12, 2013).

Mehta has no qualms to point fingers at the sacred texts of Hinduism for endorsing these oppressive customs and traditions. The opening frame of *Water* suggests how the ancient scriptures shape this despicable worldview: "A widow should be longsuffering until death, self-restraint and chaste. A virtuous wife who remains chaste when her husband has died goes to heaven. A woman who is unfaithful to her husband is reborn in the womb of a jackal" (Manu-smriti 5:156–61).[3] *Water* is obsessed with the power and mastery the sacred scriptures

---

3. This is an abridged version of the story retold by the filmmaker.

exercise in the lives of ordinary people. It often interweaves scriptural verses into dialogues in a subtle fashion. For example, when Narayan's father suggests, "Brahmins can sleep with whomever they want because the women they sleep with are blessed," Narayan's counterargument comes from another scriptural story: "Do you know what Ram told his brother? Never to honor those Brahmins who interpret the Holy Scripture for their own benefit."

In the end, Gandhi emerges as the ultimate redeemer—not only for Chuyia, but for Narayan as well—who represents the new India. He appears in the scene "from the jungles of South Africa," proposing a new method of integration between politics and religion. Narayan removes his class photo from the wall and replaces it with Gandhi's portrait, signaling that a new way of thinking has emerged in the horizon (see fig. 7.4, gallery).

Narayan is the only true Gandhian in the film, and he chooses to live a moderate life despite all the wealth he has inherited from his affluent family. In the end, he chooses to leave his real father and follow Gandhi, thus transforming his identity from being an individualist self to the nationalist whole.

Gandhi's political ideology is founded on a romantic vision of India, where people are liberated not only from political bondage, but also from the tyranny of their own cultural devices. When his friend tells Narayan, "Romantics make terrible nationalists," it also applies to the ideology he represents, Gandhism. The last spoken word in the film comes from Shakunthala as she shouts to Narayan, "Give her to Gandhi!" and she keeps reminding Chuyia, "Don't fall." In these words, Mehta shares her optimism for the future of the nation and her words of wisdom to every Indian.

The God of the Elements Trilogy

Hinduism is not one religion. No single text, Godhead, or prophet is accepted by all Hindus. Eastern religions in general, and Hinduism in particular, have an all-embracing theology with plenty of room for different worldviews, including agnosticism and even atheism. In *Water*, when Punditji reminds Shakunthala, "Don't give up faith," one might wonder "in what" or "in whom," but the Indian viewers know that this ambiguity lies at the heart of Hinduism.

The Impersonal God of Jnana Yoga

Hinduism has many schools of thought, but the most popular of all is jnana-yoga (the way of knowledge), which teaches the *advaita* (monism) philosophy. It presents God as an impersonal being, apathetic to human sufferings. Mehta's personal worldview is firmly rooted in the theological construct of jnana-yoga. When I asked if she believed in the existence of a supernatural deity, Mehta's answer was candid and honest: "I don't believe in a God figure, but I do believe that there must be a reason why we are here. . . . I believe there is something. I am still trying to figure it out. Therefore I consider myself an agnostic. I believe in spirituality. . . . That is different from God" (personal interview, June 12, 2013). This response may sound evasive or unconvincing to many, yet it is typical of the karmic worldview of jnana-yoga.

One of the basic premises of jnana-yoga is that God and human beings are essentially one and part of a universal spirit. Any apparent distinction between them is nothing but an illusion. The forces of good and evil are understood and defined by each individual based on each person's ability to comprehend the nature of this illusion. If we crave for our "self," the craving causes distress. Our aspiration must rather be to realize our oneness with the Universal Spirit, Brahman. "There is desire light and there is aspiration light," Swamiji teaches in *Fire*. "The desire light wants to devour and destroy the entire world, while aspiration light wants to feed and immortalize the whole world." Ashok puts the same truth in a different perspective as he explains it to Radha: "Desire light is the love of power. Aspirational light is the power of love." A devotee's ultimate goal is to find the true light—a spiritual process otherwise known as enlightenment.

Desire and sin interrelate in jnana-yoga.[4] According to Ashok, "Desire distracts us from the paths to God; desire is the root cause of all evil." The only thing that can help us escape the clutches of desire is abstinence. Ashok desperately seeks to attain enlightenment by renouncing all his carnal desires. "It was my destiny to achieve union with the universal truth," he muses. He has traded the pleasure of sex and taken the vow of celibacy in this pursuit. His relationship with Swamiji is stronger and more intimate than his relationship with his own wife. When Sita says, "Bhaiyya [Ashok] should fast for

---

4. The word *sin* is synonymous to ignorance in *advaita*. The real is our ignorance in failing to recognize that everything is unreal and part of the illusion.

Swamiji," she is in fact implying that the bond between the guru and the disciple has become analogous to that of the relationship between a husband and wife.

In *Water,* Narayan points out a major flaw of this worldview and its failure to relate to the lived reality of ordinary people. When Shakunthala says, "All of this is an illusion," he quickly chides her, "Kalyani's death is no illusion." If we are to subscribe to the idea that everything is an illusion and part of a cosmic whole, we will be left with no purpose for our individual lives on earth. If the universal soul and the individual souls have no personal attributes, there is no room for meaningful relationship between them. This paradox creates the proverbial "God-shaped hole" in the mind of a Hindu.

In contrast to this worldview, *Earth* makes constant reference to the evil that lies hidden deep within the human soul. Lenny is afraid that the lion in the zoo would one day break free from the cage and devour everyone. Dil Nawas, as he goes into a trance, confirms her fear through a prophecy: "At the time of division . . . you will all fight like animals." He later suggests that the fight is not just between the Hindus and the Muslims, but "it is about something inside us . . . . We are all bastards, all animals, like the lion in the zoo that Lenny is so scared of. He just lies there, waiting for the cage to open." This naked portrayal of the depravity of the human soul may find more parallels in the Pauline theology of original sin than in any philosophical constructs of Hinduism.

The Embodied God of Bhakti Yoga

Unlike the god of *Fire* and *Earth,* the god of *Water* is an embodied presence in the everyday life of his devotees. This god accepts their worship, listens to their prayers, and even enters into the miseries of their lives in a physical form. In the portrayal of this god, we see the glimpses of bhakti yoga, the devotional stream of Hinduism.

The god of bhakti yoga is not the impersonal spirit Brahman, but the personal god Iswara, who seeks spiritual communion with his creation. This god is the incarnate other, who is both transcendent and immanent at the same time. Therefore in the bhakti tradition, "the relationship between God and humans is seen as intimate and participatory and is based on local languages, literatures, performances and the arts" (Chatterji 2008: 79).

The idea of a personal god in Hindu tradition may come as a surprise to some who perceive Hinduism as a monistic or pantheistic religion. In reality, Hinduism is founded on the principle of *Sanatana Dharma,* defined by the phrase "that which exists is One: sages call it by various names" (*Ekam Sat Vipra, Bahuda Vadanti*; Rig Veda 1-164.46, Murty 2013: 13). In Rig Veda and the Upanishads, we see direct references to one supreme God. Consider the following verses:

> With eyes on all sides and mouths on all sides, with arms on all sides and feet on all sides, the One God created the sky and the earth, fanning them with his arms. (Rig Veda, 10.81.3, Coward et al. 2007: 7)

> The All-Maker is vast in mind and vast in strength. He is the one who forms, who sets in order and who is the highest image. (Rig Veda, 10.82.2, Coward et al. 2007: 8)

It is not the impersonal god of jnana-yoga, but only the personal god Ishwara of the bhakti yoga has the power to evoke religious sentiments in ordinary people's minds. Ishwara not only seeks the welfare of his creation but also intervenes in their lives in order to redeem them. This idea, according to Murthy, promotes a religion of grace, where "God is inescapable redeemer who in His infinite mercy assumes suitable forms to recover and reunite with the lost life" (Murthy 1973: 116).

N. V. George attributes this belief in a personal god to the Vaishnavite school of Hinduism, which recognizes "god as absolute from the *vedantic* point of view, yet accepts the theistic concept of a personal god who reveals himself and his will through incarnations to redeem and sustain the world" (George 1997: 57). Followers of this school believe in the concept of avatar, the descent of Vishnu from the spiritual world into the physical world in order to accomplish specific purposes. Vishnu enters the world when evil overcomes the good, and the peace and harmony of the world is threatened. In the *Bhagavad Gita,* "For protecting the good and to the destruction of evil doers for the sake of establishing righteousness I come into being from age to age" (Gita IV:8, Winthrop 1984: 208). The most popular descents of Vishnu are collectively called Dasavatara, or ten incarnations, whose stories constitute most part of the Hindu mythology.

The Elements Trilogy frames its story by drawing lavishly from some of these mythical archetypes. The leading characters of *Fire,* Sita and Radha, are named after the love interests of two epic avatars, Rama and Krishna, respectively. Rama's name is chanted Sitaram and Krishna's name Radhakrishna, implying the role of sacred romance in Hinduism.

Rama was dharma (duty) oriented, whereas Krishna was karma (action) oriented. A Hindu is encouraged to "live as Rama lived, learn what Krishna taught" (Nathan 1983: 117).

The plot of *Fire* revolves around the myth of *Agnipariksha* (The Test of Fire), a controversial episode from *Ramayana*, where Sita jumps into a fiery furnace to prove her chastity to Rama (see figs. 7.5a–b, gallery). This story is enacted in a street play, where we hear Rama saying to Sita, "I know you are pure. But I have to do my duty as a husband and put you through the test of fire." We also see the family watching the televised version of this episode in another scene. In the end, *Agnipariksha* is actualized in the climactic scene where Radha's sari catches fire and she is engulfed in flames. Ashok, like Rama, becomes a silent witness to her ordeal, but the flame cannot burn her, ironically proving the purity of her newfound love.

Krishna is the avatar that epitomizes the idea of god, who is described as the only *Poorna Avatara* (full and complete incarnation) of the Godhead (Nathan 1983: 19). In *Water*, Narayan represents the metaphorical descendant of Krishna into the dark and desolate world of the widows. When Chuyia asks Shakunthala, "Does Lord Krishna take human form?" the real answer to the question comes in the form of Narayan. Mehta depicts Narayan with obvious Krishna symbolism, often playing a flute, Krishna's favorite musical instrument (see fig. 7.6, gallery). Narayan's mischievous interactions with his mother are also representative of Krishna's playful pranks with his mother.

Radha-Krishna relationship is the supreme symbol of love in bhakti tradition, which centers around the intimacy between the gods and the devotees. "The love of Radha and Krishna is symbolic of the eternal love affair between the devoted mortal and the Divine," says Chinmayananda. "Radha's yearning for union with her beloved Krishna is the soul's longing for spiritual awakening to be united with the one Source of peace and bliss from which it has become separated" (1983: 169). Widows' devotion to Krishna is allegorical to the famous 'rasa-leela (love sport) between Krishna and his divine *gopis* (milkmaids). They are considered the brides of Krishna, a belief amplified by their constant chanting of the "Jai Krishna" mantra. Kalyani is Narayan's Radha, the most beloved *gopi*, who eventually becomes his consort. In the mythology, Krishna never married Radha; their relationship is characterized by the agony of separation. The couple was "eternally neither united nor separated" (Wright 2007: 150).

Mehta frequently calls on this mythical rendezvous between Radha and Krishna to portray the budding romance between Narayan and Kalyani. This symbolism is deliberately invoked in the song sequence "Piya Ho," which narrates Kalyani's meeting with Narayan by the water. The song starts with Kalyani worshipping the Krishna idol and slowly follows her to the riverbank, where Narayan waits for her under the banyan tree, playing a flute. The lyrics of the song resonate with many epic expressions of Radha's longing for Krishna:

Oh, my love Love.
I am carrying along full of love for you
Along with me the passion of love
You are my love in my heart, my mind
Oh, my love. I am spending the night
with your love in my mind
I am spending the light with a candle of love
From waterfront to every lane of the village
Oh dear look in my heart My eyes are thirsty
please feed me sweet love juice
My love is calling you oh my love
Listen a singing bird please find my love
Where is he, in which country? When can I meet him?

It is the same romantic notion between Krishna and Radha being invoked in *Ayo re Sakhi*, (Come, my love) which accompanies Narayan's first meeting with Kalyani. The drops of water from Kalyani's rinsed clothes fall on Narayan, morph into a drizzle, and eventually become a thundering rain. A montage of shots follows, every frame drenched in the pouring rain. The rain, like love, originates from God himself. It is pure and divine, coming down directly from the heavens, untainted by the worldly impurities. Krishna is called Karmeghavarnan in Hindu mythology, which means "the one with the color of rain clouds." Water in the form of rain symbolizes the Krishna's proclamation of love for his beloved:

My lover has come, look my friend,
The chiming sound will echo today
in the rhythm of the flute,
Lost in it the heart will dance today
with the lovesick maid
The 'koyas' has started singing its song,
The drizzle of monsoon has also begun
He has come my friend, he has come . . .
With flash and glow they dance,

the dark water laden clouds
Wrapped in the cover of monsoon,
like an enemy, the wind is blowing
The mind is filled with chiming of anklets,
The body is filled with joyous uproar of clouds

The Krishna symbolism is further reinforced in the colorful portrayal of a Holi celebration, where Chuyia is dressed up as Krishna (see fig. 7.7, gallery). According to a popular myth, the dark-skinned Krishna was jealous of the fair-skinned Radha and apparently smeared color on Radha's face to change her complexion. This prank played by Krishna later became a full-fledged festival during which people smear each other with colored powder and water guns.

Faith and Conscience

The struggle of conscience against cultural traditions is one of the recurring themes in the trilogy. In Mehta's words, "It's the whole journey of trying to understand what faith is and what it means and what oppression is. . . . That for me is the crux of the whole film. . . . It is about the conflict between conscience and faith" (personal interview, June 12, 2013).

All three films of the Elements Trilogy deal with the tyranny of ancient traditions that renders people powerless and incapacitated. These unwritten codes are deeply ingrained in the collective subconscious of the country, subtly influencing the decisions and actions each person makes in his or her life. The culture may evolve as people change, but the traditions remain frozen.

The character of Biji in *Fire* is a menacing symbol Mehta uses to portray the paralyzing force these customs and traditions exercise in the society. She is old, mute, and impotent, yet with the ominous tinkle of a bell, she dictates the actions of everyone else in the household. Like Ashok, who chooses to hold on to Biji instead of rescuing his wife from imminent death, people succumb to its power even when they have the opportunity to break free. Sita alludes to this predicament as she wonders, "Isn't it amazing that we are so bound by customs and rituals! Somebody just has to press a button, this button marked tradition. And I start responding like a trained monkey."

In *Water*, Chuyia's father is heartbroken when he walks away from his daughter, who is now confined to the ashram. It is certainly not a willful act, nor is it motivated by any malicious intent, but he is simply following the tradition like a "trained monkey." When Narayan discloses his intention to marry a widow, his mother's immediate concern is "What will people say?" All these characters are imprisoned in a cage like Madhumathi's parrot, and they have lost the power to break free even when the opportunity presents itself.

The apparent disparity between the voice of conscience and the voice of faith, according to Mehta, is caused by the misappropriation of the sacred texts by religious leaders. The powerful aristocrats and the priestly class at the pinnacle of the social hierarchy manipulate the true message of the scriptures to serve their self-interests. When Shakunthala wonders why the news about the widow remarriage did not reach the ashram, Pundit responds candidly, "We ignore the laws that don't benefit us." In the words of Narayan's friend, "Avoid widows, slippery steps and holy men. Liberation awaits."

It is also interesting to note that Mehta does not discredit the role of religious practitioners, however. In *Fire*, Swamiji is the spiritual adviser to Ashok, whose decisions and actions are central to the narrative. Jathin detests Swamiji's invisible presence in the family and disapproves of Ashok's decision to extend financial support to him, but he eventually comes to realize the good in Swamiji. In *Earth*, the Imam becomes a symbol of rebellion when he swears a blatant lie in the name of Allah in order to save the life of a Hindu woman. In *Water*, Pundit is a fellow pilgrim who is also torn by the conflict between faith and conscience.

It is also interesting to note that the customs and traditions are not considered evil in themselves. Even Kalyani, one of the most tragic victims of this social evil, is prudent enough to recognize their cultural significance. When Narayan says, "All the old traditions are dying out," Kalyani's response is immediate: "But what is good should not die out." Conflict between conscience and faith is resolved only in the enlightened mind of an individual. "Who will decide what is good and what is not?" asks Narayan. Kalyani's answer points us straight to the core message of the film: "You." What holds the key to social reformation is the transformation of an individual's heart. It is the moral compass of a believer that determines the authenticity of his or her faith.

From Pundit's conversation with Shakunthala, we are aware of the fact that reformation is already under way and the remarriage of widows has become legal. But legislation is powerless against the stigma attached to a tradition. The power to change the course of social drama lies within the psyche of each actor, not in the legal structures of social institutions. The only way out of the conundrum is the transformation of the individual self, when everyone decides to choose the voice of conscience over that of faith. As Narayan decides to follow Gandhi, leaving his father's inheritance behind, Shakunthala also makes a radical decision to break free from the bondage of the ashram and to become an agent of change.

It is important to remember that by "faith," Mehta means religious rules and regulations, not the belief in God or the practice of spiritual disciplines. However, her understanding of "conscience" is rather complicated, especially when we look at this construct from other theological perspectives. For example, while the dichotomy between faith and conscience exists in Christian tradition, faith is sustained through pure conscience.[5] All humans are bestowed with a conscience,[6] which acts as a guide to deciding between right and wrong. God has embedded a priori moral codes in the deep recesses of human conscience. Therefore, conscience becomes the "innate thrust of our human nature to love good and avoid evil" (Fagan 1997), which eventually leads us to true faith. In Pauline theology, the voice of conscience becomes the voice of faith when it is guided by the Holy Spirit, and the law becomes inscribed in our hearts. This "hermeneutics of the Spirit" helps us interpret the scripture in order to construct true religion in social conscience.

What if the voice of faith and voice of conscience contradict? Obviously, Mehta presumes that our conscience is morally neutral and we need to listen to its prompting. But the voice of conscience is not formed in isolation. Richard Gula argues that conscience is created by three features of human nature: All humans are born with a conscience that has the "capacity" to know what is good, which has to be formed and shaped through a "process" of intersection with different moral standards. As the conscience evolves, it also involves "judgment" of action based on individual circumstances, where decisions are made based on available information (Gula 1989). In other words, conscience is a continuous evolutionary process, being purified through the culture (and the scripture). The conscience is not a product of culture, but it is still conditioned by one's cultural environment.

In Eastern religions, when individual conscience experiences

5. "They must keep hold of the deep truths of the faith with a clear conscience" (1 Tim 3:9); "keeping faith and a good conscience, which some have rejected and suffered shipwreck in regard to their faith" (1 Tim 1:19).
6. See Rom 2:14–15.

"enlightenment," the true nature of the reality is revealed to the self. This heightened state of conscience is similar to Kohlberg's idea of "post-conventional level of conscience" (Kohlberg 1976), where an individual desires the greatest good of the greatest number of people. Such an individual assumes a separate identity from the society and reinterprets the existing social norms and values based on his or her individual conscience. Individuals derive their own moral codes, which are superior to that of the society, and override the rules inconsistent with these codes. The rules of tradition may be a useful mechanism to maintain social equilibrium, but they can be transformed by a postconventional conscience. In light of this principle, great souls like Jesus, the Buddha, or even Gandhi are categorized as people with a pure state of conscience, which has the capacity to discern between the moral right and wrong.

This is where we find the significance of Gandhi, who is introduced as a mythical figure that invites a theological conversation. Mehta portrays him as an otherworldly character, with the camera keeping a reverential distance from his face. The presence of the divine in the film is experienced through the perfection of humanity in Gandhi. The theological center of the trilogy lay in the tension of being true to one's belief while at the same time trying to be true to one's humanity. The famous Vaishnava mantra, which lingers in the background during Gandhi's appearance in the train station, is one of the classic representations of ideal human in Hindu sacred texts:

He who understands the pain of others is a Vaishnavite.
  Helping others in need, he does not gloat in pride.
This person respects all people in the world,
  and does not condemn or criticize anyone.
  He is pure in speech, deed and thought.
Mother of such person is blessed indeed!
He is equanimous and has given up all desires.
To him, other women are [equivalent to] mothers.
He or she never speaks a lie, and does not covet others' wealth.
Delusion and attachment do not affect him or her,
  with mind firm in detachment.
Such a person is ever engrossed in meditation of God,
  and embodies all places of pilgrimage.
Such a person has no greed or deceit,
  and has overcome lust and anger.
Such a person is worthy of worship.

Gandhi was the epitome of ideal humanity who taught that true divinity could be found only in true humanity. It is his prophetic voice that brings resolution to the conflict between faith and conscience in the trilogy. For Mehta, Gandhi is the bridge between humanity and divinity.

Unlike the popular version of humanism in the West, Gandhi's humanistic ideal is theistic, with a strong emphasis on the worship of God through the service of humanity. The discovery of true humanity within us is the starting point of spirituality. He believed that all "human beings are working consciously or unconsciously towards the realization of spiritual identity" (Parida 2000: 20) and looked upon men and women as the manifestations of God. It is through this deep focus on Gandhi's humanity that Mehta brings resolution to the conflict between conscience and faith. His vision of life, therefore, can be appropriated to a transcendent experience in our religious criticism of the trilogy.

Summary

In the final shot of *Water*, Shakunthala turns around and looks at the audience. She has now learned that true faith comes not from sacred texts written in parchments, but from the invisible words written in her conscience. In the struggle between faith and conscience, ultimate victory belongs to the conscience of an individual. This, in essence, is the message of the trilogy.

Shakunthala's gaze transcends time and space, demanding from us a religious response conditioned by our own struggles between faith and conscience. Her eyes penetrate our emotional core, "compelling us to reflect, among other things, on a particular indignity of our own situation" (Mahadevan 2007: 175). I realize that my own (Christian) tradition needs to reexamine its history through this critical lens provided by the trilogy. Christendom has also used its sacred text to justify social evils such as crusades, inquisitions, slavery, and even discrimination against women. Today, as we are confronted with new questions on moral and political correctness, one might wonder at which point is it appropriate to listen to the voice of conscience over the voice of tradition.

Although the Elements Trilogy is set in the context of India, beneath the surface level it is targeting the general dysfunction that exists within the sociocultural system of every society. Even when the story is taking place in a particular time and in a particular place, the core issues discussed in the trilogy resonate with viewers of all religious faiths and cultural backgrounds. In her invitation to experience the tension between the voice of faith and that of conscience, Mehta's religious criticism thus transcends cultural borders and achieves universal significance.

8

___

Conclusion

The art of storytelling has progressed over the years from oral to written forms and eventually into audiovisual formats. In the digital age we live in, Film has become not only the most popular form of mass entertainment, but also a powerful medium for cultural reflection and exchange. According to Gordon Gray, film is where the "grand discourses" take place and the dialogue between "political economy and globalization, class and gender and internationalism versus nationalism [which] intersect with the lives of everyday people" (Gray 2010: 140).

In our world, film has emerged as a mirror of culture, which reflects how the social lives of people are interconnected through various modes of relationship. Film not only reflects the culture, but also acts as a powerful agency of change in shaping social norms, values, and even worldview assumptions. The impact of film may be felt immediately on tangible aspects of culture such as fashion, etiquette, and lifestyle, but it also has a subtle influence on the intangible aspects of culture, such as ideals, beliefs, and value systems. Film's role in creating social awareness and forming public opinion is of particular interest in our interconnected world.

We are witnessing revolutionary changes in the field of communication technology, which is considerably reducing the cost of film production, making the process cheaper, simpler, and faster. Independent films with lower production budgets are finding larger audiences and winning more awards and accolades at prestigious film festivals. This is redefining the relationship between art and business in the industry, enabling film to become a medium for authentic expressions of the human condition. It provides us "not only with a new venue in which to investigate the human condition, but also an arena where so much of the unspoken (ideologies, taste and distinction, and other forms of embedded culture) come out on display" (Gray 2010: xvi).

Ethnographic investigation of cinema is a vital yet underused tool in religious studies. In this book, I have proposed a methodology for reading religious information from film by applying both theological and anthropological insights into film criticism. The proposed methodology is a synthesis of the dialogical method in theological criticism of film (chapter 2) and a new methodology for the cultural exegesis of film (chapter 3).

We start religious criticism by looking into the artistic structure of the film using traditional film analysis. At least a cursory understanding of the theology of the dominant religious belief system of the context is important in analyzing the substantive dimension of religion manifested in the film. We examine the diegetic world of the film for the functional aspects of religion through cultural exegesis—a process in which the ethnographic data embedded in the filmic world is extracted with due consideration given to the subjectivity of the filmmaker and the influence exercised by the filmmaking context. Methodology for cultural exegesis consists of an interlacing of auteur criticism and context criticism, two methods borrowed from the discipline of film studies, with virtual participant observation, an eclectic combination of participant observation and film analysis.

We used the Elements Trilogy—an Indo-Canadian film series consisting of *Fire* (1991), *Earth* (1998), and *Water* (2005)—as a case study to test this methodology. We compared and contrasted ethnographic data generated from the trilogy through virtual participant observation with the actual data collected from the field to test the authenticity of film's re-presentation of culture. The field research involved participant observation, focus groups, and ethnographic interviews conducted in India and an interview with Deepa Mehta, the writer/director of the film series. The field research unearthed various ways in which the ethnographic content represented in a film can be influenced by the auteur of the film and the context of its production. We also discovered that although the religious content of the trilogy is specific to its cultural context, its message is universal. The film series has a panhuman quality with etic and emic representations of the culture, which can also find resonance in films of other cultures.

The methodology for religious criticism of film we applied to the case study can be extended to cinemas around the world. It provides a framework to observe and interpret the perception of "the religious" in any cultural context by looking at a film from that culture with an anthropological lens on one eye and a theological lens on the other. The criticism does not pass judgment on a film's moral quality or aesthetic superiority, but it focuses mainly on its capability to provide authentic ethnographic information and its ability to enter into a dialogue with the theology of its context.

The methodology proposed in this book should enable the students of religion and film to connect the secular in anthropology with the sacred in theology to create a more holistic religious reading of film. I hope they will gain a renewed appreciation for the religious diversity of our global village by learning to decode the ethnographic representation in world cinema. This process will become instrumental in initiating a mutually informative trialogue between film, culture, and theology in the field of religious studies.

Appendix 1

Ethnographic Films

It is generally believed that an aboriginal kangaroo dance and rain ceremony, shot by Baldwin Spencer on April 2, 1901, was the first ethnographic film ever recorded. However, the art of ethnographic filmmaking was first celebrated when Robert Flaherty released *Nanook of the North* in 1922. This feature-length documentary portrayed the life of an individual, Nanook, in his cultural setting, where the ethnographic knowledge unfolded through a dramatic narrative. Ironically, many scenes that were considered to be authentic cultural depictions were staged for the camera and shot on the set because of the practical difficulties in shooting on location. The film was widely discussed for "its authenticity, its fakery, its romanticism" (MacDougall 1998: 103).

Ethnographers tend to prefer the apparent realism of documentary films to the "fictitious" narratives constructed by feature films. The world represented by a documentary film is presumably the "real world" around us, though the overlap of the real and fictive might be stronger than suggested. In documentary films, reality is a mechanical reproduction of the real world, where the subjects and their cultural behavior are depicted as they are. It has to be recognized, however, that any effort to create an ethnographic present is fictional and often pretentious, according to the postulates of postmodern anthropology. "Documentary film cannot help participating in the codes and conventions of fictional cinema, even as it signals its genre differences," note Devereaux and Hillman. "Documentary film takes place within the (maternal) body of fictional cinema, which is itself involved in a dance with European conventions of how to tell stories and what stories are there to tell" (Devereaux and Hillman 1995: 330).

Peter Crawford (1992) suggests "observational cinema," a blend of documentary and fictional cinema, as a better reflection of ethnographic film, on account of its emphasis on objectivity, neutrality, and transparency. In the "observational" style of filmmaking, the filmmakers make themselves socially invisible to attribute ethnographic authority to the narrative. The subjects assume a noninteractive stance with the viewers or the filmmakers. The style observes "life as it is and leaves the interpretation of its codes open to the viewers." Based on this definition, films such as *The Box* (2004), *Schoolscapes* (2007), *Sheep Rushes* (2007), and *High Trail* (2007) are considered "ethnographic" by virtue of their subject matter. Heider in the same vein identifies Satyajit Ray's narrative feature-film series the Apu Trilogy—*Pather Panjali* (1955), *The Unvanquished* (1956), and *The World of Apu* (1959)—as "masterpieces of what might be called ethnographic fiction" (2006: 27).

The role of narrative feature film as a medium of cultural representation has been a highly stigmatized and controversial topic in the field of visual anthropology. Heider writes that "in some sense one could argue that all films are 'ethnographic': they are about people" (2006: 4). Jay Ruby, in contrast, vehemently opposed "the tendency on the part of some anthropologists to equate virtually any film about people with ethnography," and considered it "a serious impediment to the development of a social scientific means of visual communication" (1975: 105). At the same time, he also believes that film "as a medium and technology of communication has the potential for the communication of scientific statements." The filmmaker's objective is to present a believable cultural framework for the diegetic world of the film, whereas an anthropologist focuses on exploration of the world through the camera. Though "all films may be potentially useful to anthropologists," not all of them can be considered ethnographic in the traditional sense. An ethnographic film should be subjected to the same criteria for scientific examination that are applied to other ethnographic documentations, and the filmmakers are obliged to maintain anthropological precision in the production process.

According to Ruby (1975), for an ethnographic film to be considered an authentic form of cultural representation, it must meet the following criteria:

- The primary concern of the work should be the description of a whole culture or some definable element of a culture. So the exclusive purpose of an ethnographic film is the generation of ethnographic knowledge, not an artistic exploration of the culture.

- An ethnographic work must be informed by "an implicit or explicit theory of culture, which causes the statements within the work to be organized in a particular way" (Ruby 1975: 107). The selection of events for filming, the method of filming, and the editing of the images will reflect the theory adopted by the filmmaker.

- An ethnographic film must also reveal the methodology used in collecting, analyzing, and organizing the data. The methodology of the filmmaker marks an important difference between film as an artistic medium to explore culture and film as a scientific tool for the study of culture.

- Any ethnographic work must employ a distinctive lexicon, which Ruby describes as an "anthropological argot." Anthropologists are trained to employ the linguistic codes of the observed culture, which enables them to distinguish between works of ethnography and works with ethnographic intent.

The creators of ethnographic films, in Ruby's opinion, have so far not developed a method for presenting images in the framework of a code or argot. Until they develop these codes, their products can be considered films about anthropology, not "anthropological films." That being said, Ruby agrees to the idea that an anthropologist has the liberty to examine any film for ethnographic information, assuming that it preserves information of the past from historical events or changing social conditions of the present. A strong caution should be exercised against the blind acceptance of feature films as a means for communicating ethnography, of course, but all films have research utility in anthropological education.

MacDougall, in the same vein, describes "modern" ethnographic films as open-ended "texts" in that they incorporate and juxtapose multiple perspectives of the researcher, informants, and subjects (MacDougall 1998). Therefore researchers must possess the aesthetic sensibilities of a filmmaker and the scientific mind of an anthropologist. They should be disciplined to think within the bounds of a theoretical framework while also allowing a free flow of creative imagination to construct the diegetic world.

Carl Heider, in his classic book *Ethnographic Film*, lists sixteen qualitative scales to measure the "ethnographicness" of a film (Heider 2006):

1. **Appropriateness of sound.** The sound track may involve music, natural sound, narration, etc., but should be used only to reinforce the information provided by the visual.
2. **Narration.** Narration should not be used to carry a story line; rather it should be sparse and closely related to the visual.
3. **Ethnographic basis.** The film should be a product of scientific ethnographic research, which calls for the active involvement of an ethnographer.
4. **Explicit theory.** The film should incorporate anthropological theories in the analysis of social organization.
5. **Relation to printed materials.** The film should be supplemented with written ethnographic materials.
6. **Voice.** Though many points of view may be used to analyze the situation, it should remain as objective as possible.
7. **Behavioral contextualism.** The audience may pick up what they choose from the visuals and interpret that information their own way. So there should be a great emphasis on the context of behavior to exploit the capacity of film to picture the whole.
8. **Physical contextualization.** The film should depict where the action really takes place.
9. **Reflexivity.** The film should acknowledge the presence of the ethnographers and filmmakers in the scene.
10. **Whole acts.** Selection of shots should be done so as to present the important features of an act, i.e., beginning, middle, and climax.
11. **Narrative stories.** The film should maintain continuity for the shots, following its storyline.
12. **Whole bodies.** Though focusing on specific part of the body can intensify the purpose, the use of close-ups should be generally avoided.
13. **Whole interactions.** Personal interactions in ethnographic films are generally low, and the emphasis should be more on people doing physical activities.
14. **Whole people.** It is recommended to focus on whole people (individuals) rather than faceless masses.
15. **Distortion in the filmmaking process.** It has to be recognized that the film is a subjective medium, and it distorts, alters or select images of reality in many ways. A distortion of behavior could be inadvertent, where the presence of a camera makes a natural difference in the response of the people or intentional

distortion of behavior that involves triggering or staging a behavior or interrupting a behavior for a better camera shot.

16. **Culture change made explicit.** An effort to create an ethnographic "present" in a film is purely fictional, because culture is evolving continuously.

Today postmodern theoreticians have opened up new ways of looking at ethnography as a "thick description" of culture, guided by the implicit narrative structure of a story. A narrative feature film, therefore, can function as a cultural document that provides valuable ethnographic information of its context. In other words, all films can be considered a "datum of culture" from which ethnographic data can be extracted and analyzed, even when the film in itself may not be categorized as an ethnographic film.

Appendix 2

Christ Figures in Film

A Christ figure is essentially an "allegory [that] follows the main thread of the Christ story, while disguising it through a surface narrative. . . . The figure is strong enough to exist by itself, but points to a meaning far beyond this existence for its ultimate truth" (Holloway 1977: 187). Christ figures can be disguised as women, clowns, or even animals (*Au Hazard Balthazar* 1966). They need not always be religious themselves, yet they draw on the "universal cultural symbolic value of the Jesus persona" (Hurley 1982:66).

Baugh (1997) describes Christ figures as "cinematographic foils of Jesus," which can be unearthed by reading the "sacred subtexts" embedded within a film narrative. Most recognizable Christ figures sacrifice themselves in order to save others. Two readily recognizable Christ figures are John Coffey in *Green Mile* (1999) and Babette in *Babette's Feast* (1987). John Coffey is an innocent prisoner on death row, convicted of a crime he did not commit. He heals the sick, awakens the dead, and even shares Jesus Christ's initials (JC). Babette demonstrates how renunciation and indulgence can coexist in our lives, as in the life of Jesus, a Nazirite monk who was often accused of being a winebibber. She is the epitome of sacrificial giving that gives till the giver becomes exhausted and extinguished. Other commonly cited examples of films with Christ figures are *Shane* (1953), *Dead Man Walking* (1995), *Bicycle Thieves* (1948), *The Passion of Joan of Arc* (1928), and *One Flew over the Cuckoo's Nest* (1975).

Baugh even pushes the argument further and attributes revelatory powers to Christ figures. "The person and the situation of the Christ figure can provide new understanding of who and how Christ is," argues Baugh. "Jesus himself is revealed anew in the Christ figure" (1997: 112). Whatever we learn from the Christ figure in a film is considered a new revelation of Christ.

The search for Christ figures has been criticized as showing "either the banality of the category itself or the desperation of theologians to find connections with modern culture" (Pope 2005: 174). According to Marsh, "The quest for Christ figures in literature and film is a tired (and sometimes tiresome) pastime . . . [that] borders on triteness" (Marsh 2004: 51). In Deacy's opinion, "To assume that something about Christ's activity is straightforwardly transferable to the realm of modern-day cinematic Christ figures is to necessitate an insupportable leap of faith" (Deacy 2008: 139).

However, Johnston considers the Christ-figure approach legitimate, based on the premises of myth criticism. A Christ figure can be considered a cultural archetype in our collective consciousness—a product of the subconscious theological memory in our culture. "In certain films, a Christ figure is a primary metaphor or the Christ story does function significantly as a defining theme giving shape to the narrative," argues Johnston. "When this is the case, any criticism of the movie that fails to notice this theme is an incomplete criticism" (Johnston 2006: 69). If film reflects archetypical characters from timeless mythologies, it is natural to assume that such "god figures," "savior figures," or "prophet figures" can be found in world cinema. This is how we understand the "Krishna figure" in Narayan's character in *Water*.

Appendix 3

Film Analysis

The term *film analysis* refers to the process of unpacking the meaning of a film by extrapolating the text, image, and sound within a cinematic event.[1] In film, all three components come together to tell a "story," which will be the focal point of film analysis. Story is the narrative engine that holds the three components together. The sensory components are critiqued in terms of how they affect the story, not based on their individual merits.

Narrative

Narrative is the essential structure of the story, which gives meaning to various events happening in the plot. According to Johnston (2000), the sequence of these events is organized around four essential components: plot, point of view, characters, and atmosphere.

The plot is a device with which the filmmaker orchestrates the key events in the story. It is the basic structure of the narrative within which the story takes place. A typical plot involves the journey of a protagonist in search of his or her desire. A conflict arises when the antagonist confronts the protagonist to exert opposition to the journey. Also, a plot can be built around the mental, emotional, and moral conflicts of the protagonist. In some plots, both protagonist and antagonist can be the same; a person becomes his or her own worst enemy. The antagonist can also be an impersonal force—for example, the forces of nature in *Life of Pi* (2012) or religious fundamentalism in

---

1. The methodology for film analysis described in this appendix is based on Prunes et al. (2002), Johnston (2000), and Bywater and Sobchack (1989).

United 93 (2006). When the protagonist figures out a way to resolve the conflict, the plot moves to resolution. The cycle of conflict resolution drives the narrative forward and keeps the viewers engaged in the film.

A film's point of view determines the perspective through which it tells the story. Filmmakers persuade the viewers to watch the film through a particular "eye," whether that of an outsider or any of the characters in the film. Watching the story unfold through the eyes of a particular character limits the information available to the viewers. But it also helps focus viewers' attention, allowing new perspectives to emerge. A filmmaker may use selective points of view as a dramatic device to create suspense, by letting the viewers speculate on the missing information. In some films, the narrative may be mediated through a narrator, who stands between the filmmaker and the characters. The viewer's discernment of the narrator's point of view controls the meaning of the story.

The third element of the narrative is character. Characters are the agents that carry out actions that advance the plot. These actions reveal the character traits. A change in character trait over the course of a narrative is known as a "character arc." Great characters undergo radical changes in their behavior or attitude from the beginning to the end of the story; hence they have a better character arc. Such characters are often called dynamic or round characters because they possess a variety of conflicting and contradictory traits. They are active in their response to the plot and multidimensional in their personality. Characters that are one-dimensional with only one dominant, constant trait are called static or flat characters. These characters are shallow and predictable because their traits do not change in relation to the events of the narrative.

The fourth element of the narrative is the atmosphere, which defines the given qualities of the environment within which the characters operate. Atmosphere is a metaphorical borderline for the plot; it determines the boundary for the events that take place in the narrative. The atmosphere is closely connected to the setting of the film in which the story takes place. The characters in a Holocaust film, such as *Life Is Beautiful* (1997) or *Schindler's List* (1993), are limited by the inhumane rules of the Nazi regime, whereas the hiker in *127 Hours* (2010) and Pi in *Life of Pi* (2012) are limited by the forces of nature.

A narrative is often organized according to themes or series of themes, which give significance and meaning to the actions that take place in the narrative. The theme can be explicit or implicit. It provides insight into the underlying meaning, or the moral of the story.

Image

The second component of the filmic story is image. A shot-by-shot analysis of the film can become an exhaustive and cumbersome process. Therefore, for practical purposes, we look at three essential components that constitute a movie's image: mise-en-scène, cinematography, and editing.

"Mise-en-scène" represents all the things that are put in the scene to create a frame. It includes the sets, the decor, the lighting, the costumes, and at times, the performance of the actors. Films often use the elements of mise-en-scène to intensify or to undermine the significance of a particular scene. The decor may be used to amplify character emotions or the mood of the film. The intensity, direction, and quality of lighting affect the way images are perceived. Lighting affects the way colors are rendered and can draw attention to specific elements of the composition. Costumes signify character, promote particular fashions, or make distinctions between various characters. Depth, proximity, size, and proportions of the places and objects in a film can be manipulated through mise-en-scène components, redefining the relationships between various elements in the filmic world.

Cinematography determines the composition of an image by defining its balance of dark and light, the depth of the space in focus, the relation of background and foreground, and so on. The Yale *Film Analysis Guide* (Prunes et al. 2002) describes cinema as an "art of selection," which makes framing a key concept in cinematography. The edges of the image create a frame that includes or excludes aspects of what occurs in front of the camera. Framing techniques include the angle of the camera to the object, the aspect ratio of the projected image, the relationship between camera and object, and the association of camera with character. Innovative filmmakers use different techniques in cinematography to manipulate viewers' perception of the context and the characters. The contrast between light and dark is often used metaphorically to distinguish between good and evil. A deep focus—staging an event such that the significant elements occupy widely separated planes in the image—can be used to achieve a truer representation of space. A shallow focus can be used to suggest psychological introspection—for example, when a character appears oblivious to the world. The angle of framing can be used to indicate the relation between characters and the camera's point of view, or it can be used to create striking visual compositions from different perspectives.

Different filmic devices can be used to convey the subjective experience of the characters. Some realist filmmakers, for example, try to use camera shots from eye level in order to let the viewers experience the events in a real-life viewing situation. Others use different camera angles to stimulate or manipulate viewers' empathy with the characters. When a tilted camera is used at a lower level to shoot a fallen soldier, for example, it gives the viewer a psychological identification with the fallenness of the character. The camera angles can thus help simulate multiple voices, allowing polyvocal modes of presentation, solving to a large extent the problem known as the "crisis of representation" in postmodern terms.

Editing is a process of sequencing the images to create the flow of scenes in the narrative. It can affect viewers' experience of time in the diegetic world by creating a gap between the screen time and the "diegetic time." It can also establish a fast or slow rhythm for the scene—the perceived rate and regularity of sounds, series of shots, and movements within the shots, and so on. According to Browne, "the process of joining the shots brings yet other processes of signification; meaning is created by the juxtaposition of shots and the impact upon audience is demonstrable" (Browne 1998: 16).

Instead of presenting film as a perfectly self-contained story that seamlessly unfolds in front of the viewers, innovative filmmakers employ different editing techniques to create powerful emotional connections with the story. For example, a sudden freeze of frame interrupts the narration and grabs the curiosity of the audience. Slow motion creates drama, whereas fast motion creates comedy. Computer-generated imagery (CGI) characters create magical realism. A transition technique, such as dissolve, can be used to indicate a time lapse in narration or even to suggest a hallucinatory state of a character. A montage emphasizes dynamic, often discontinuous, relationships between the shots to create ideas not present in either shot by itself. A cut-in or cut-away creates visceral effects by forcing an instantaneous shift from a distant framing to a closer view of some elements for the same space, and vice versa. A jump cut suggests the characters' ruminations or ambivalence. These are some of the many ways in which editing can function as a powerful tool for creating images to which viewers respond voyeuristically, vicariously and viscerally.

Sound

Sound in film is classified into diegetic and nondiegetic sound, depending on its relationship between the world of the characters and that of the viewers. Diegetic sound originates within the film's world, whereas nondiegetic sound is represented as coming from a source outside the story space. Any voice, musical passage, or sound effect presented as originating from a source within the film's world is diegetic sound. In other words, the source of diegetic sound is visible on the screen or implied to be present by the action of the film (voices of characters, sounds made by various objects in the story, or music represented as voices of the characters). If the sound originates outside the film, then it is nondiegetic. Its source neither is visible on the screen nor has been implied to be present in the action; examples include a narrator's commentary, sound effects added for dramatic effect, and background music. The sound can also be off-screen or on-screen. A voiceover, for example, is used to give a sense of character's subjectivity or to narrate an event told in a flashback. Some filmmakers might even intentionally mismatch voiceover narrations over the images to reveal the unreliable or deceptive nature of the characters.

In a film, the sound track is typically divided into three categories: dialogue, sound effects, and music. According to Buhler, "Everything depends on the dialectic the music establishes with the image track on the one hand and with dialogue and effects in the sound track on the other" (2001: 58).

In *Film Music*, Larsen explains how music functions in the context of the narrative, aesthetic, and psychological functions of the film. He suggests that music can be approached as an accompaniment to film, or film can be considered as an illustration of the music. The exploration of this relationship between film and music enables us to discover new facets of the narrative (Larson 2005: 35). The rhythm of a film is intrinsically connected to the music. Rhythm contributes to the mood created by the film and its overall impression on spectators. The right rhythm is achieved through a complex combination of film and sound editing. In some cases, filmmakers may choose to compose the music first and a scene is shot to fit that rhythm later, reversing the traditional order. The sound in a film is also used to define space in the diegetic world. A film can register the space in which sound is produced, or manipulate audience perception of the space and mood for dramatic purposes. The sense of a sound's position in space, yielded by volume, timbre, and pitch in multitrack reproduction systems, creates a more realistic sense of space, with events happening closer or farther away.

The sound is designed to match the genre of the film by creating a certain level of expectation about its content for the audience. Slobin notes the role music plays in genre criticism: "Music signals genre, such as comedy, horror film, western, or thriller, even before you grab your first handful of popcorn. This system relies on well known codes attached to specific musical instruments, orchestration, special effects. . . . This entire really complicated system of signs and subtexts goes down easily" (2009: viii). Getter and Bala observe how the use of certain instruments can create a setting in time and place, as well as a pace for the action and an emotional feeling. Instrumental timbre (tone quality) is significant in signaling important ideas to the audience. "A particular raga (melodic mode) can quickly set a certain mood, a folk rhythm can establish a rural scene, or a techno beat can evoke a modern character or milieu" (Getter and Bala 2008: 121).

Here are some helpful questions to ask while doing film analysis:

1. What is the genre of the film? How does it use or transgress the traditional conventions of genre?
2. How does the construction of the plot direct our interpretation of an event?
3. Who is the protagonist? Who is the antagonist? Why are the antagonist and the protagonist in conflict?
4. What does the outcome of the conflict reveal about the protagonist's journey? Did you feel sympathetic to the protagonist or antagonist?
5. What are the main characters? Why do they behave in specific ways? What does each character contribute to the narrative?
6. Is the characterization round or flat? What is the character arc?
7. How well did the actors perform their roles? How are the experience and inner life of the characters presented?
8. What are the givens in the story? What are the unchangeable conditions under which the characters operate?
9. What is the point of view, or perspective? Is there a narrator? Does the point of view limit our knowledge of the story?
10. What are some of the unifying themes in the narrative?
11. How do elements such as style, images, and symbols contribute to the meaning of the story?

12. What does the mise-en-scène tell us about the world in which the story takes place?
13. How do the camera's point of view and its movement, angle, shot composition, etc. influence the diegetic process?
14. What are the editing devices used? Do they try to manipulate the viewer's perception?
15. What is the role of music in this film? What are the tempo and rhythm? Do they distract us or enhance our experience?
16. How does the sound differ in the diegetic and nondiegetic worlds?
17. Do the lyrics convey cultural meanings? Do they belong to an ethnic, folk, or traditional collection of the culture in which the film is produced?

Bibliography

Armes, Roy. 1997. *Third World Film Making and the West.* Berkeley: University of California Press.

Baartmans, Frans. 1990. *APAH, The Sacred Waters: An Analysis of a Primordial Symbol in Hindu Myths.* Delhi: B. R. Publishing.

Bandy, Mary, and Antonio Monda. 2003. *The Hidden God: Film and Faith.* New York: Museum of Modern Art.

Banks, Marcus. 1995. "Visual Research Methods." *Social Research Update*, no. 11, Winter.

____. 2001. *Visual Methods in Social Research.* London: Sage.

____. 2002. "Visual Research Methods." *Indian Folklife*, vol. 1, no. 4, p. 3.

____. 2007. *Using Visual Data in Qualitative Research.* London: Sage.

Barbour, Rosaline. 2007. *Doing Focus Groups.* London, Sage.

Basset, Stefania. 2012. "The Dislocated Woman in Deepa Mehta and Meena Alexander's Works." *Frontiers and Cultures 2011: Europe and the Americas, Intra and Intercontinental Migrations,* Venice: Studio LT2, March, 14–25.

Baugh, Lloyd. 1997. *Imaging the Divine: Jesus and Christ-Figures in Film.* Kansas: Sheed & Ward.

Bergesen, Albert, and Andrew Greeley. 2000. *God in the Movies.* New Brunswick, NJ: Transaction.

Bernard, H. Russell 2006. *Research Methods in Anthropology: Qualitative and Quantitative Approaches.* Lanham, MD: Altamira.

Boorstin, Jon. 1995. *Making Movies Work: Thinking Like a Filmmaker.* Los Angeles: Silman-James.

Brant, Jonathan. 2012. *Paul Tillich and the Possibility of Revelation through Film.* London: Oxford University Press.

Browne, David. 1998. "Film, Movies, Meaning." Marsh and Ortiz, 9–20.

Bryant, Darrol M. 1982. "Cinema, Religion, and Popular Culture." *Religion in*

Film, edited by John R. May and Michael Bird. Knoxville: University of Tennessee Press, 101–14.

Buhler, James. 2001. "Analytical and Interpretive Approaches to Film Music." *Film Music: Critical Approaches*, edited by K. J. Donnelly. Edinburgh, Edinburgh University Press, 51–62.

Bywater, Tim, and Thomas Sobchack. 1989. *An Introduction to Film Criticism: Major Theoretical Approaches to Narrative Film*. New York: Longman.

Chatterjee, Gautam. 1996. *Sacred Hindu Symbols*. New Delhi: Abhinav.

Chatterjee, Madhuri. 2007. "Women's Bodies, Women's Voices: Exploring Women's Sensuality in Deepa Mehta's Trilogy." Jain 2007b, 75–84.

Chatterji, Gayatri. 2008. "Designing a Course on Religion and Cinema in India." Watkins, 77–117.

Chaudhuri, Shohini. 2009. "Snake Charmers and Child Brides: Deepa Mehta's *Water*, 'Exotic' Representation, and the Cross-Cultural Spectatorship of South Asian Migrant Cinema." *South Asian Popular Culture*, vol. 1, no. 7.

Chen, Martha A. 2000. *Perpetual Mourning: Widowhood in Rural India*. New York: Oxford University Press.

Chinmayananda, Swami. 1983. "Radha and Krishna." *Symbolism in Hinduism*, edited by R. S. Nathan. Bombay: Central Chinmaya Mission Trust.

Cho, Francisca. 2003. "The Art of Presence: Buddhism and Korean Films." *Representing Religion in World Cinema*, edited by B. S. Plate. New York: Palgrave Macmillan.

Clifford, James. 1988. *The Predicament of Culture: Twentieth Century Ethnography, Literature, and Art*. Cambridge, MA: Harvard University Press.

Clifford, James, and George Marcus, eds. 1986. *Writing Culture: The Poetics and Politics of Ethnography*. Berkeley: University of California Press.

Coward, Harold, Newufeldt, Ronald and Neumaier, Eva eds. 2007. *Readings in Eastern Religions*. Waterloo: Wilfred Laurier University Press.

Craughwell, Kathleen. 1999. "Movies Grounded to 'Earth': Political Upheaval in 1947 India Is the Subject of the Second Film in Director Deepa Mehta's Trilogy." *Los Angeles Times*, September 9, p. F10.

Crawford, Peter. 1992. "Film as Discourse: The Invention of Anthropological Realities." *Film as Ethnography*, edited by P. I. Crawford and D. Turton. Manchester: Manchester University Press.

Cunneen, Joseph. 2003. *Robert Bresson: A Spiritual Style in Film*. New York: Continnum International.

Datta, Vishwa Nath. 1998. *Sati: A Historical, Social and Philosophical Enquiry into the Hindu Rite of Widow Burning*. New Delhi: Manohar.

Deacy, Christopher. 2001. *Screen Christologies: Redemption and the Medium of Film*. Cardiff: University of Wales Press.

_____. 2005. *Faith in Film.* Hampshire, UK: Ashgate.

_____. 2008. "The Pedagogical Challenges of Finding Christ Figures in Films." Watkins, 129–41.

Deacy, Christopher, and Gaye Ortiz. 2008. *Theology and Film: Challenging the Sacred/Secular Divide.* Malden, MA: Blackwell.

Detweiler, Craig. 2007. "Seeing and Believing: Film Theory as a Window into a Visual Faith." *Reframing Theology and Film,* edited by R. K. Johnston. Grand Rapids: Baker Academic.

Devereaux, Leslie, and Roger Hillman, eds. 1995. *Fields of Vision: Essays in Film Studies, Visual Anthropology and Photography.* Berkeley, CA: University of California Press.

Dhavamony, Mariasusai. 2002. *Hindu-Christian Dialogue: Theological Sounding and Perspectives.* Amsterdam: Rodopi.

Dwyer, Rachel. 2000. *All You Want Is Money, All You Need Is Love: Sexuality and Romance in Modern India.* New York: Cassel.

_____. 2006. *Filming the Gods: Religion and Indian Cinema.* New York: Routledge.

Ebert, Roger. 1995. "Camilla Movie Review." *RogerEbert.com,* March 24, www.rogerebert.com/reviews/camilla-1995. Accessed December 9, 2014.

Eck, Diana L. 1998. *Darshan: Seeing The Divine Image in India.* New York, Columbia University Press.

_____. 2002. "Darshan." *Religion, Art, and Visual Culture,* edited by Brent Plate. New York: Palgrave, 171–75.

Erndl, Kathleen. 2000. "Is Shakti Empowering for Women? Reflections on Feminism and the Hindu Goddess." *Is the Goddess a Feminist?: The Politics of South Asian Goddesses,* edited by K. M. Erndl and A. Hiltebeitel. New York: Sheffield.

Fagan, Sean. 1997. *Does Morality Change?* Dublin: Gill & Macmillan.

Ganti, Tejaswini. 2012. *Producing Bollywood.* Durham, NC: Duke University Press.

Geertz, Clifford, ed. 1971. *Myth, Symbol and Culture.* New York: W. W. Norton.

_____. 1973. *The Interpretation of Cultures.* New York: Basic Books.

_____. 1983. *Local Knowledge: Further Essays in Interpretive Anthropology.* New York: Basic Books.

George, N. V. 1997. *The Doctrine of Incarnation in Vaishnavism and Christianity.* Delhi: ISPCK.

Gerstner, David. A. 2003. "The Practices of Authorship." *Authorship and Film,* edited by D. A. Gerstner and J. Staiger. New York: Routledge.

Getter, Joseph, and Subrahmanian Bala. 2008. "Tamil Film Music: Sound and Significance." *Global Soundtracks: Worlds of Film Music,* edited by M. Slobin. Middletown, CT: Wesleyan.

Gire, Ken. 1996. *Windows of the Soul: Experiencing God in New Ways.* Grand Rapids: Zondervan.

Gray, Gordon. 2010. *Cinema: A Visual Anthropology.* Oxford: Berg.

Gula, Richard. 1989. *Reason Informed by Faith.* New York: Paulist.

Harris, Gardiner. 2013. *Charges Filed Against 5 Over Rape in New Delhi.* The New York Times. New York: The New York Times. January 3, 2013.

Hawthorn, Jeremy. 2006. "Theories of the Gaze." *Literary Theory and Criticism,* edited by P. Waugh. London: Oxford University Press.

Heider, K. G. 2006. *Ethnographic Film.* Austin: University of Texas Press.

Heinz, Caroline B. 1999. "Kanyadan: Gift of a Virgin." The Maithil Brahmans: An Online Ethnography. Retrieved April 7, 2016, from www.csuchico.edu/anth/mithila/kanyadan2.htm.

Hill, John, and Gibson, Pamela, eds. 2000. *World Cinema: Critical Approaches.* New York: Oxford University Press.

Hurley, Neil P. 1982. "Cinematic Tranfigurations of Jesus". *Religion in Film.* edited by J. R. May and M. Bird. Knoxville: University of Tennessee Press, 61–78.

Iser, Wolfgang. 1993. *The Fictive and the Imaginary: Charting Literary Anthropology.* Baltimore, MD: Johns Hopkins University Press.

Jain, Jasbir. 2002. *Films and Feminism: Essays in Indian Cinema.* New Delhi: Rawat.

_____. 2007a. "The Diasporic Eye and the Evolving I: Deepa Mehta's Element Trilogy," in Jain 2007b, 54–74.

_____. 2007b. *Film, Literature and Culture: Deepa Mehta's Element Trilogy.* New Delhi: Rawat.

Jain, Madhu, and Sheela Raval. 1998. "Ire over Fire." *India Today,* December 21, 1998. http://indiatoday.intoday.in/story/controversial-film-fire-is-sent-back-to-censor-board-matter-taken-to-court/1/265473.html.

Jodha, Avinash. 2007. "Packaging India: The Fabric of Deepa Mehta's Cinematic Art." Jain 2007b, 39–53.

Johnston, Robert K. 2006. *Reel Spirituality: Theology and Film in Dialogue.* Grand Rapids: Baker.

Khorana, Sukhmani. 2009a. "Diasporic Art: Writing/Visualising Back and Writing/Visualising into Being." *Communication, Creativity and Global Citizenship.* Brisbane: University of Adelaide.

_____. 2009b. "Maps and Movies: Talking with Deepa Mehta." *Bright Lights Film Journal,* vol. 63, January 31.

Kirkland, Paul. 1997. "Deepa Mehta Takes on the Customs of India in the First of Three Works." *Toronto Sun.* Toronto.

Kohlberg, Lawrence. 1976. "Moral Stages and Moralization: The Cognitive-Developmental Approach." *Moral Development and Behavior: Theory, Research and Social Issues,* edited by L. Kohlberg and T. Lickona. New York: Rinehart & Winston.

Kothari, Sweety. 2013. "100 years of Indian cinema." http://newsonair.nic.in/100-YEARS-OF-INDIAN-CINEMA.asp. Accessed October 30, 2014.

Kracauer, Siegfried. 1960. *Theory of Film: The Redemption of Physical Reality.* Princeton, NJ: Princeton University Press.

Kumar, Nitin 2003. *Ganga The River Goddess Tales in Art and Mythology.* Retrieved December 11, 2015, from http://www.exoticindiaart.com/article/ganga/.

Kumar, Sandeep. 2012. "Humanism in Gandhian Philosophy." *International Indexed and Refereed Research Journal,* vol. 3, no. 32, p. 2.

Lamb, Sarah. 2000. *White Saris and Sweet Mangoes.* Berkeley: University of California Press.

Larsen, Peter. 2005. *Film Music.* London: Reaktion.

Lyden, John. 2003. *Film as Religion.* New York: New York University Press.

_____. 2008. "Teaching Film as Religion." Watkins, 209–19.

MacDougall, David. 1998. *Transcultural Cinema.* Princeton, NJ: Princeton University Press.

Mahadevan, Uma. 2007. "Readings, Misreadings and Fundamentalist Readings: Reflections on the Making of Deepa Mehta's *Water.*" Jain 2007b, 168–76.

Majumdar, Bandana. 2009. *Widows, Renunciation, and Social-Self: A Study of Bengali Widows in Varanasi.* New Delhi: Manak.

Malinowski, Bronislaw. 1961. *Argonauts of the Western Pacific.* New York: E. P. Dutton.

Marsh, Clive. 1998. "Film and Theologies of Culture." Marsh and Ortiz, 21–34.

_____. 1998. "Religion, Film and Theology in a Postmodern Age: A Response to John Lyden." *Journal of Religion and Film,* vol. 2, no. 1.

_____. 2004. *Cinema and Sentiment: Film's Challenge to Theology.* Waynesboro, GA: Paternoster.

_____. 2008. "Is It All about Love Actually? Sentimentality as Problem and Opportunity in the Use of Film for Teaching Theology and Religion." Watkins, 155–65.

_____. 2009. "Theology and Film." *The Continnum Companion to Religion and Film,* edited by W. L. Blizek. London: Continnum.

Marsh, Clive, and G. Ortiz, eds. 1997. *Explorations in Theology and Film.* Malden, MA: Blackwell.

Martin, Joel W., and Conrad E. Ostwalt Jr., eds. 1995. *Screening the Sacred: Religion, Myth, and Ideology in Popular American Film.* Boulder, CO: Westview.

Mera, Miguel, and Anna Morcom. 2009. "Introduction: Screened Music, Transcontextualisation and Ethnomusicological Approaches." *Ethnomusicology Forum,* vol. 18, no. 1, p. 17.

Miles, Margaret. 1996. *Seeing and Believing: Religion and Values in the Movies.* Boston: Beacon.

Mukherjee, Tutun. 2007. "Deepa Mehta's Film *Water*: Constructing the Dialectical Image." Jain 2007b, 218–32.

Murthy, Srinivasa. 1973. *Vaishnavism of Sankaradeva and Ramanuja*. Varanasi: Motilal.

Nagib, Lucia. 2006. "Towards a Positive Definition of World Cinema." *Remapping World Cinema: Identity, Culture and Politics in Film*, edited by Stephanie Dennison and Song Hwee Lim. New York: Wallflower.

Nathan, R. S., ed. 1983. *Symbolism in Hinduism*. Bombay: Central Chinmaya Mission Trust.

Nayar, Sheila J. 2012. *The Sacred and the Cinema: Reconfiguring the 'Genuinely' Religious Film*. London: Continuum.

Niranjana, Tejaswini, and Mary E. John. 1999. "Mirror Politics: Fire, Hindutva and Indian Culture." *Economic and Political Weekly*, March 6–13, 81–84.

Nye, Malory. 2003 *Religion: The Basics*. London: Routledge.

O'Flaherty, Wendy D., ed. 1975. *Hindu Myths: A Source Book Translated from Sanskrit*. Middlesex, UK: Penguin.

Ostwalt, Conrad. 2008. "Teaching Religion and Film: A Fourth Approach." Watkins, 35–57.

Panjwani, Narendra. 2006. *Emotion Pictures: Cinematic Journeys into the Indian Self*. New Delhi: Rainbow.

Parameswaran, Uma. 2007. "Problematising Diasporic Motivation: Deepa Mehta's Films." Jain 2007b, 10–22.

Parida, Gunanidhi. 2000. *Ecology and Development in Conflict: A Gandhian Approach*. New Delhi: APH Publishing.

Patil, Godavari D. 2000. *Hindu Widows: A Study in Deprivation*. New Delhi: Gyan.

Phillips, R., and W. Alahakoon. 2000. "Hindu chauvinists block filming of Deepa Mehta's *Water*." www.wsws.org/en/articles/2000/02/film-f12.html.

Plate, S. Brent, ed. 2002. *Religion, Art, and Visual Culture*. New York: Palgrave.

——, ed. 2003. *Representing Religion in World Cinema: Film Making, Myth Making, Culture Making*. New York: Palgrave Macmillan.

——. 2008a. "Film Making and World Making: Recreating Time and Space in Myth and Film." Watkins, 219–32.

——. 2008b. *Religion and Film: Cinema and the Recreation of the World*. London, Wallflower.

——. 2009. "Religion and World Cinema." *The Continnum Companion to Religion and Film*, edited by W. L. Blizek. London: Continnum.

Pope, Robert. 1995. "Salvation in Celluloid: Theology, Imagination and Film." London: T&T Clark.

Prasad, Madhava M. 1998. *Ideology of the Hindi Film: A Historical Construction*. Delhi: Oxford University Press.

Prunes, Mariano, Michael Raine, and Mary Litch. 2002. "Yale Film Studies: Film Analysis Website 2.0." *Film Analysis Guide*, August 27, filmanalysis.yctl.org/. Accessed October 31, 2014.

Pungente, John. 2005. "Water." *Scanning The Movies*. D. Robinson. Toronto, Bravo Network: 42:00.

Rai, Sudha. 2007. "The Diasporic Gaze: Deepa Mehta's and Bhapsi Sidhwa's *Water*." Jain 2007b, 201–17.

Ramanamma, A., and Debjani P. Chaudhari. 2004. "Widows in Maharashtra: Perspectives, Strategies and Rehabilitation." *Problem of Widows in India*, edited by A. P. Reddy. New Delhi: Sarup & Sons.

Ramchandani, Vinita. 1998. "Passionate Plots." *The Week (Bombay)*, December 6, p. 27.

Reporter. 2000. *VHP: shooting of 'Water' not to be allowed*. Chandigrah: The Tribune. February 5, 2000. http://www.tribuneindia.com/2000/20000205/main4.htm.

Roy, Rakhi, and Jayasinhi Jhala. 1992. "An Examination of the Need and Potential for Visual Anthropology in the Indian Social Context." *Visual Anthropology and India*. Calcutta: Anthropological Survey of India.

Ruby, Jay. 1975. "Is an Ethnographic Film a Filmic Ethnography?" *Studies in the Anthropology of Visual Communication*, vol. 2, no. 2, Fall.

_____. 2000. *Picturing Culture: Explorations of Film and Anthropology*. Chicago: University of Chicago Press.

Schechner, Richard. 1985. *Between Theater and Anthropology*. Philadelphia: University of Pensylvania Press.

_____. 1990. "Magnitudes of Performance." *By Means of Performance: Intercultural Studies of Theater and Ritual*, edited by R. Schechner and W. Appel. Cambridge: Cambridge University Press.

_____. 2003. *Performance Theory*. London: Routledge.

Schrader, Paul. 1988. *Transcendental Style in Film*. Cambridge: Da Capo Press.

Shankar, R., M. Thamilarasan, and V. Umadevi. 2004. "Widows in Rural Setting: A Sociological Study." *Problem of Widows in India*, edited by A. P. Reddy. New Delhi: Sarup & Sons.

Singh, Vijay. 2007. "Exteriority, Space and Female Iconography in Mehta's *Water*." Jain 2007b, 189–200.

Sison, Antonio D. 2012. *World Cinema, Theology and the Human: Humanity in Deep Focus*. New York: Routledge.

Slobin, Mark, ed. 2008. *Global Soundtracks: Worlds of Film Music*. Middletown, CT: Wesleyan University Press.

_____. 2009. "Central Asian Film Music as a Subcultural System." *Ethnomusicology Forum*, vol. 18, no. 1, 153–64.

Snigdha, Madhuri. 2012. "Women's Bodies as Sites of Signification and Contestation: An Analysis of Deepa Mehta's Critique of Narratives of Home, Nation and Belonging in the Elemental Trilogy." Master's thesis, University of British Columbia.

Thomas, Rosie. 1985. "Indian Cinema, Pleasures and Popularity." *Screen*, May–August vol. 26, no. 3/4.

Tillich, Paul. 1973. *The Boundaries of Our Being.* London: Collins.

____. 1987. *On Art and Architecture.* New York: Crossroad.

____. 2011. *On the Boundary: An Autobiographical Sketch* Eugene: Wipf & Stock.

Turner, Harold. 1981. "The Way Forward in the Religious Study of African Primal Religions." *Journal of Religion in Africa*, vol. 12, no. 1, 1–15.

Turner, Victor. 1967. *The Forest of Symbols: Aspects of Ndembu Ritual.* New York: Cornell University Press.

____. 1974. *Dramas, Fields, and Metaphors: Symbolic Action in Human Society.* New York: Cornell University Press.

Turner, Victor. 1979. *Process, Performance, and Pilgrimage: A Study in Comparative Symbology.* New Delhi: Concept.

____. 1982. *From Ritual to Theatre: The Human Seriousness of Play.* New York: Performing Arts Journal Publications.

____. 1985. *On the Edge of the Bush: Anthropology as Experience.* Tucson: The University of Arizona Press.

Varadarajan, Siddharth. 2000. "The BJP and Deepa Mehta's 'Water': Strife as Diversion and Design." *Times of India*, February 26.

Vasudev, Aruna. 1986. *The New Indian Cinema.* Delhi: Macmillan.

"VHP, RSS Say No to Shooting *Water*." 2000. *Indian Express (Bombay)*, February 5.

Virdi, Jyotika. 2003. *The Cinematic imagiNation: Indian Popular Films as Social History.* New Brunswick, NJ: Rutgers University Press.

Watkins, Gregory J. 2008. *Teaching Religion and Film.* New York: Oxford University Press.

____. 2009. "Religion, Film and Film Theory." *The Continnum Companion to Religion and Film*, edited by W. L. Blizek. London: Continnum.

Wikinson, Sue. 1999. "How useful are Focus Groups in Feminist Research," in *Developing Focus Group Research: Politics, Theory and Practice,* edited by J. Kitzinger and R. S. Barbour. London: Sage, 64–78.

Winthrop, Sargeant. 1984. *The Bhagavad Gita: Revised Edition.* Albany: State University of New York Press.

Woodward, Mark R. 1996. "Hermeneutics." *Encyclopedia of Cultural Anthropology*, edited by D. Levinson and M. Ember. New York: Henry Holt, 555–58.

Wright, Melanie J. 2007. *Religion and Film: An Introduction.* New York: I. B. Tauris.

Subject Index

Film Index